MODERN WARFARE

THE GULF WAR

CW01471654

NEWHAM LIBRARIES

90800100215281

Civilians and coalition military forces wave Kuwaiti and Saudi Arabian flags as they celebrate the liberation of Kuwait. The use of 'all necessary means' had only driven Saddam back and while he remained in power the suffering continued in Iraq until 2003.

MODERN WARFARE

THE GULF WAR

*Operation Desert Storm
1990–1991*

Anthony Tucker-Jones

Pen & Sword
MILITARY

First published in Great Britain in 2014 by
PEN & SWORD MILITARY
an imprint of
Pen & Sword Books Ltd,
47 Church Street,
Barnsley,
South Yorkshire
S70 2AS

Text copyright © Anthony Tucker-Jones, 2014
Photographs copyright © as credited, 2014

ISBN 978 178159 391 2

The right of Anthony Tucker-Jones to be identified as Author of this
Work has been asserted by him in accordance with the Copyright,
Designs and Patents Act 1988.

A CIP record for this book is available from the British Library.

All rights reserved. No part of this book may be reproduced or
transmitted in any form or by any means, electronic or mechanical
including photocopying, recording or by any information storage and
retrieval system, without permission from the Publisher in writing.

Typeset by CHIC GRAPHICS

Printed and bound in Malta by Gutenberg Press Ltd

Pen & Sword Books Ltd incorporates the imprints of Pen & Sword
Archaeology, Atlas, Aviation, Battleground, Discovery, Family
History, History, Maritime, Military, Naval, Politics, Railways, Select, Social
History, Transport, True Crime, and Claymore Press, Frontline Books,
Leo Cooper, Praetorian Press, Remember When, Seaforth Publishing
and Wharncliffe.

For a complete list of Pen & Sword titles please contact
Pen & Sword Books Limited
47 Church Street, Barnsley, South Yorkshire, S70 2AS, England
E-mail: enquiries@pen-and-sword.co.uk
Website: www.pen-and-sword.co.uk

Contents

Preface

Pen & Sword's Modern Warfare series is designed to provide a visual account of the defining conflicts of the late twentieth and early twenty-first centuries. These include Operations Desert Storm, Iraqi Freedom and Enduring Freedom. A key characteristic of all three, fought by coalitions, is what has been dubbed 'shock and awe', whereby superior technology, air supremacy and overwhelming firepower ensured complete freedom of manoeuvre on the ground in the face of a numerically stronger enemy. The focus of this series is to explain how military and political goals were achieved so swiftly and decisively.

Another aspect of modern warfare is that it is conducted in the full glare of the international media. This is a trend that started during the Vietnam War, and today every aspect of a conflict is visually recorded and scrutinized. Such visual reporting often shapes public perceptions of conflict to a far greater extent than politicians or indeed generals.

All the photographs in this book, unless otherwise credited, were issued by the US Department of Defense and the UK's Ministry of Defence at the time of the conflict. The author and the publishers are grateful for the work of the various forces' combat photographers.

A Syrian soldier guarding his base. Syria provided an armoured division equipped with Soviet-designed tanks to defend Saudi Arabia.

Introduction

In response to Saddam Hussein's invasion of Kuwait in 1990, the US instigated Operation Desert Shield, a massive multi-national effort to defend Saudi Arabia in the event of Saddam advancing further south. The Coalition feared Saddam would attack Saudi Arabia's vital oilfields, and initially there was very little to stop him. However, once America began her build-up in Saudi, Saddam showed his hand by withdrawing those forces – the Republican Guard and Regular armoured divisions – that were capable of attacking the border.

Operation Desert Sabre – the ground war to liberate Kuwait from Iraqi occupation in 1991 – culminated in one of the largest tank battles since the Second World War, and was certainly Britain's largest armoured action since then. It was a historic moment, for despite the demise of the Cold War, the American M1A1 Abrams and British Challenger tanks finally engaged the Soviet-designed T-72 and T-62 main battle tanks.

Quite remarkably, after a ground war lasting just four days the Iraqi Army of Occupation was reduced to no more than seven operational divisions out of an original total of forty-three, and 15 per cent of Iraq was under coalition control. In particular, Saddam's powerful armoured formations had not lived up to their fearsome reputation as portrayed by the West. This was in part due to the Coalition's crushing air power deployed during the aptly named Operation Desert Storm, but the Iraqi ground forces' poor combat performance must also be attributed to inadequate direction from Baghdad.

At the start of the war a line was drawn in the sand as the Iraqis adopted overtly defensive positions. The Republican Guard straddled the Iraqi–Kuwaiti border to form a strategic armoured reserve, though some also moved to Baghdad to defend the regime against external or internal threats. This left insufficient Iraqi forces facing the Coalition along the Saudi border, resulting in less capable conscripts in under-strength divisions being stretched over a wide front. This presented a logistical nightmare for the Iraqi high command, especially after Coalition air forces began to attack their exposed lines of communication.

The US-led Coalition gathered half a million men from thirty-one countries, comprising nine US divisions, one British, one French and four Arab. They were equipped with 3,400 tanks and 1,600 pieces of artillery. The Arab states of the Gulf Co-operation Council only deployed 10,000 men, though in the Gulf region they had 150,000 men and 800 tanks available.

Saddam's armed forces could not be underestimated or even dismissed. By 1990 the Iraqis were estimated to have 5,500 tanks, 8,100 APCs, 500 self-propelled guns and 3,200 pieces of artillery and multiple rocket launchers. Whilst it is impossible to account for all these, visible deliveries of Iraqi armoured vehicle imports between 1953 and 1990 number at least 3,500 MBTs and 5,200 AFVs. During the late 1970s and 1980s Iraq had bought considerable quantities of weaponry from Brazil, China, Czechoslovakia, Egypt, France and the USSR. Notably at the time even Brazil had a thriving wheeled armoured vehicle industry and did good business with Iraq.

Initially, while the USSR dithered over the issue of neutrality in the Iran–Iraq War, China and Egypt had moved swiftly to fill the vacuum left with Iraq. In fact China and Czechoslovakia, in the name of impartiality and good business, sold weapons to both sides. Moscow, not wanting to miss out, resupplied Iraq but when the Iran–Iraq War was over cynically sold tanks and APCs to Iran.

Despite a decade of buying weapons with which to fight the Iranians, the Iraqi armed forces were a paper tiger: their intimidating reputation was more legend than reality, despite their massive manpower and powerful air and armoured forces. Their military standing was not as significant as had been made out, and during the Iran–Iraq War they performed barely adequately. Iranian incompetence saved Saddam more than Iraqi military flair.

However, within the Iraqi armed forces the Republican Guard Corps (RGC) was highly regarded and received preferential treatment in terms of equipment and pay. During the Iran–Iraq conflict it formed a strategic reserve, fighting in most of the major battles. Expanding from one armoured brigade in 1980 to three armoured, one infantry and one commando by the late 1980s, by the time of the invasion of Kuwait it was claimed the RGC consisted of seven powerfully equipped divisions with some of the latest Soviet tanks.

Once the ground war commenced on 24 February 1991, the Iraqis quickly abandoned Kuwait City, as US Marine feints convinced them that they faced amphibious assault from the Gulf. Their flight from the Kuwaiti capital began on the night of 25 February and the roads north to Basra became jammed. The next day about a thousand Iraqi vehicles on Highway 80 were destroyed by air strikes after the Muttla Pass was blocked.

By early March Saddam only had left about 700 of the 4,500 tanks and 1,400 of the 2,800 APCs deployed in the Kuwaiti Theatre of Operations (KTO) and with organized resistance over, he quickly agreed to a cease-fire. While Desert Storm was an outstanding military victory, the peace was flawed as Saddam Hussein was left in power for another twelve years.

Saddam's 'Hands of Victory' – twin triumphal arches were erected to mark his victory over Iran, the Iran–Iraq War was in fact a bloody stalemate.

A close up of Saddam's hands. These ironically were cast in the UK and the monument was dedicated just before the invasion of Kuwait.

Saddam's likeness was everywhere in Iraq.

Another enormous monument to Saddam's costly war with Iran, the blue tiled split dome is covered in sand. His invasion of Kuwait unleashed a new kind of desert storm upon Iraq.

Chapter One

Desert Shield

After his disastrous and fruitless eight-year war with Iran, in the late 1980s President Saddam Hussein decided to distract public attention away from the economic and political failings of his regime by embarking on a new foreign adventure. He planned to reclaim Iraq's lost province – oil-rich Kuwait. The catalyst for his invasion was a spurious row over oil production, but it served its purpose. The tension was rapidly cranked up to breaking point.

Saddam's military build-up was swift. On 15 July 1990 a Republican Guard division of 10,000 men and 300 tanks moved just north of Kuwait. Four days later three divisions of 35,000 men deployed 16km from the border. By 27 July these forces had swelled to an overwhelming eight divisions numbering 100,000 troops. Many observers mistook this build-up for bellicose posturing, dismissing the idea that, after the exhausting decade-long conflict with Iran, Saddam would embark on yet another war so soon. They were quickly proved wrong.

Saddam's Medina and Hammurabi Divisions, two powerful Republican Guard Corps armoured units, invaded Kuwait on 2 August 1990. The following day the Tawakalna Republican Guard Division moved to secure Kuwait's border with Saudi Arabia, sealing off the country from the outside world. Approximately 140,000 Iraqi soldiers and 1,800 tanks poured into Kuwait. In the face of such military muscle there was no hope of the Kuwaitis defending themselves.

The Kuwaiti Army, not fully mobilized to its standing strength of just 16,000 men, was swiftly overwhelmed. Prior to the Iraqi invasion, Kuwait's armoured holdings included 70 old British Vickers Mk1 tanks, 40 Centurions, 165 Chieftains and 6 Yugoslav M-84s. Some 224 examples of the latter, Soviet T-72s built under licence, were still on order and had they been delivered Saddam might have thought twice.

Only around the Emir's palace in Kuwait City itself was there any extensive resistance, lasting about two hours. The small Kuwait Air Force briefly attacked the Iraqi armoured columns swarming over the country but its base was quickly overrun. The Iraqis seized 4 Kuwaiti Mirage jet fighters, 12 Hawk trainers, 5 A-4 Skyhawks, 4 C-130s, 2 DC-9s, 2 Gulfstream 111s and 43 helicopters. Kuwait found itself under Saddam's control within the space of just twelve hours. The Arab states of the Gulf Co-operation Council (GCC) and the rest of the international community were aghast. The invasion of Kuwait seemed a precursor to a much wider war.

Saddam appointed Ali Hassan al-Majid as the *de facto* governor of Kuwait and Alaa Hussein Ali as the prime minister of the puppet provisional government of Free Kuwait. The former was known as 'Chemical Ali' after his extensive use of chemical weapons against Iraq's Kurds in the late 1980s, which culminated in the infamous attack on Halabja. His appointment caused great alarm amongst coalition intelligence circles for it seemed to confirm Saddam's intention to use chemical weapons to defend Kuwait. Although al-Majid was recalled to Baghdad in November 1990, it was not before the troops under his command had systematically looted Kuwait of everything they could lay their hands on, and had driven out large numbers of the population.

On 28 August 1990 Kuwait was formally annexed and transformed into the Kuwait Governorate, Iraq's 19th province. Alaa Hussein Ali disingenuously remarked, 'Kuwait is now ours, but we might have refrained from taking such a decision if US troops were not massed in the region with the threat of invading us.' Kuwait had been part of Basra province during the days of the Ottoman Empire, and Saddam felt it only right that he take it back. The Iraqi Revolutionary Command Council declared: 'The free provisional Kuwaiti government has decided to appeal to kinsfolk in Iraq, led by the knight of Arabs and the leader of their march, President Field Marshal Saddam Hussein, to agree that their sons should return to their large family, that Kuwait should return to the great Iraq – the mother homeland – and to achieve complete merger unity between Kuwait and Iraq.'

In the wake of the invasion, western and Arab states were quick to deploy forces to defend Saudi Arabia. Since the 1973 Arab–Israeli War, Saudi pre-eminence had increased, for while it lacked significant military manpower, it played a significant role in the Organization of Petroleum Exporting Countries (OPEC) as the leading producer. Despite being a feudal society divided by Islamic dogmatism and liberalization, Saudi Arabia's security remained (and remains) a priority for the West as it has the largest proven oil reserves in the world. Kuwait was vital as a buffer zone between Saudi Arabia and its volatile neighbours to the north and east.

In the early 1980s the fear was that fundamentalist Shia Iran could easily overwhelm the combined Sunni Arab states of the GCC. Ironically the Saudis and Kuwaitis 'loaned' Saddam Hussein in excess of $50 billion for his war effort against Iran during the 1980s, and Saudi volunteers fought in the Iraqi armed forces. Now Saddam was threatening Saudi Arabia's security and sending oil prices spiralling.

On 7 August 1990, in response to the invasion five days earlier, the United States Air Force's (USAF) 1st Tactical Fighter Wing deployed with forty-eight F-15 jets from

Langley Air Force Base (AFB) in Virginia to Saudi Arabia as part of Operation Desert Shield. Poised to fly defensive missions within hours of arriving, they commenced combat air patrols along the Iraqi frontier three days later. The enemy stayed out of the way until on 11 November 1990 an Iraqi MiG-25 brazenly crossed the Saudi border, but flew back before any action was taken. As hostilities had not officially commenced, it was felt prudent not to shoot it down.

On 11 September 1990 US President H.W. Bush addressed a joint session of Congress:

> In the early morning hours of 2 August, following negotiations and promises by Iraq's dictator Saddam Hussein not to use force, a powerful Iraqi army invaded its trusting and much weaker neighbour, Kuwait. Within three days 120,000 Iraqi troops with 850 tanks had poured into Kuwait and moved south to threaten Saudi Arabia. It was then that I decided to act to check that aggression.
>
> At this moment, our brave servicemen and women stand watch in that distant desert and on distant seas, side by side with the forces of more than twenty other nations. . . .
>
> Our objectives in the Persian Gulf are clear, our goals defined and familiar: Iraq must withdraw from Kuwait completely, immediately and without condition. Kuwait's legitimate government must be restored. The security and stability of the Persian Gulf must be assured. And American citizens abroad must be protected. These goals are not ours alone. They have been endorsed by the United Nations Security Council five times in as many weeks. Most countries share our concern for principle. And many have a stake in the stability of the Persian Gulf. This is not, as Saddam Hussein would have it, the United States against Iraq; it is Iraq against the world.

President Bush then instigated Operation Desert Shield, a massive multi-national effort to defend Saudi Arabia. Major General Houston's US 82nd and Major General James H.B. Peay III's 101st Airborne Divisions arrived in August 1990. The US 24th Infantry (Mechanized) Division, in the shape of its 1st and 2nd Brigades under Major General Barry McCaffrey, was the first heavy formation to deploy to the Gulf in September 1990. It was followed by Brigadier General John Tilelli's US 1st Cavalry Division the following month and Major General Thomas Rhame's US 1st Infantry Division (Mechanized) in December. All these units had come from America and, with the exception of the 3rd Armored Cavalry Regiment, were equipped with the M1 or IPM1 Abrams tank armed with a 105mm gun.

Due to the collapse of the Warsaw Pact and the negligible threat posed by the

USSR, Washington was also able to redeploy Major General Ronald Griffith's 1st Armored and Major General Paul Funk's 3rd Armored Divisions from Germany to bolster Desert Shield. These units were equipped with the newer improved M1A1 tank with a Rheinmetall 120mm M256 gun.

By late January 1991 there were well over half a million US personnel from all services in theatre. The number of US ground forces committed to Desert Shield and the subsequent operations (Desert Storm and Desert Sabre) under General H. Norman Schwarzkopf to liberate Kuwait was staggering: approximately 260,000 troops equipped with about 2,000 M1A1 tanks and 2,200 M2 and M3 Bradley infantry fighting vehicles, supported by 500 artillery pieces plus 190 Apache and 150 Cobra attack helicopters. There were also 90,000 Marines with 200–300 M60 tanks, 250 light armoured vehicles, 430 amphibious assault vehicles and 160 aircraft.

Britain committed 35,000 men under Lieutenant General Sir Peter de la Billière, including the 1st British Armoured Division under Operation Granby. This comprised the 7th Armoured Brigade (the 'Desert Rats'), with two regiments of FV4030 Challenger Mk 3s, and the 4th Armoured Brigade plus another regiment, totalling 160 tanks commanded by Major General Rupert Smith. The division's three mechanized infantry battalions were each equipped with forty-five new FV510 Warrior mechanized combat vehicles. The two reconnaissance units were equipped with a range of vehicles based on the Scorpion.

France contributed 14,000 men, as part of Opération Daguet, under Lieutenant General Michel Roquejoffre, who commanded the French Rapid Reaction Force. The French force comprised Foreign Legion, Marine infantry, helicopter and armoured car units. The main formation was the 6th Light Armoured Division, with forty AMX-10C AFVs under Brigadier General Mouscardes. It should be noted that French divisions are smaller than their NATO counterparts and are typically reinforced brigades. However, the 6th Division was augmented with reinforcements that included the 4th Dragoon Regiment, a tank unit equipped with forty-four AMX-30B2 tanks, from the French 10th Armoured Division. Although the AMX-30B2 model was old and due to be replaced by the Leclerc, it was more than able to deal with most Iraqi tanks.

The Kuwaiti Army in exile consisted of three or four brigades, totalling 10–15,000 men, equipped with over sixty Chieftain and M-84 tanks. The principal armoured unit was the 38th Kuwaiti Armoured Brigade, dubbed the 'Al Shadid' or Martyrs. It had lost twenty-two of its eighty Chieftains during the Iraqi invasion. The 35th Kuwaiti Mechanized Brigade was equipped with M113 tracked APCs.

Saudi contributed two main forces: the regular Saudi Arabian Armed Forces (SAAF) and the Saudi Arabian National Guard (SANG). By 1991 the SAAF totalled 67,500 men, the army or Royal Saudi Land Forces (RSLF) fielding 40,000 of them, organized into two armoured, four mechanized (including the 10th Armoured, and the 8th, 10th, 11th and 20th Mechanized Brigades), one infantry and one airborne brigade, equipped with 550 tanks (including 300 French AMX-30s and 250 American M60s) and 1,840 combat vehicles, APCs and armoured cars. SANG totalled 55,000 men with 35,000 active troops and 20,000 tribal levies, equipped with 1,100 American V-150 Commando APCs.

The largest Arab contingent, comprising some 47,000 troops, came from Egypt. It consisted of the 3rd Mechanized Division (with about 200 M60s, 300 M113 APCs and M109 self-propelled guns) and the 4th Armoured Division (with about 250 M60s and 250 M113s and M109s). Syria committed 19,000 men, consisting of one airborne brigade and the 9th Armoured Division (with 250 T-62 and T-72 tanks plus BMP IFVs). In return for its support Syria received $1 billion from Saudi Arabia. Both Egypt and Syria stated that their troops were only to be deployed to defend Saudi Arabia, though this attitude was to change. Qatar also provided an armoured battalion equipped with about twenty-four French-supplied AMX-30 tanks. In total the Coalition gathered half a million men from thirty-one countries armed with 3,400 tanks and 1,600 pieces of artillery, while the allied air forces included 1,736 combat aircraft and 750 support aircraft.

General Schwarzkopf was an experienced pair of hands. Commissioned in 1956, he had served as an adviser and then as a battalion commander during the Vietnam War and was highly decorated for his exploits. He was a divisional commander during the invasion of Grenada in 1983. Five years later Schwarzkopf assumed command of US Central Command or CENTCOM based in Tampa, Florida, with responsibility for military operations in the Middle East, North Africa and Central Asia. Supporting him were Lieutenant General John Yeosock, commanding the US Army forces deployed for Desert Shield and Desert Storm, Vice Admiral Stan Arthur, commanding the US Navy forces in the Gulf, Lieutenant General Chuck Horner, commanding the US Air Force in the Gulf, and Lieutenant General Walt Boomer, commanding the US Marines in the Gulf.

Despite the massed array of military hardware and repeated calls by the United Nations for Iraq to withdraw, Saddam Hussein refused to leave Kuwait. In the face of such obstinacy, the Coalition prepared its plans for a ground war, but first, under the guise of Operation Desert Storm, coalition fighter-bombers were to hunt down every piece of Iraqi military equipment they could find. What followed was a largely uncontested air war – some likened it to a turkey shoot.

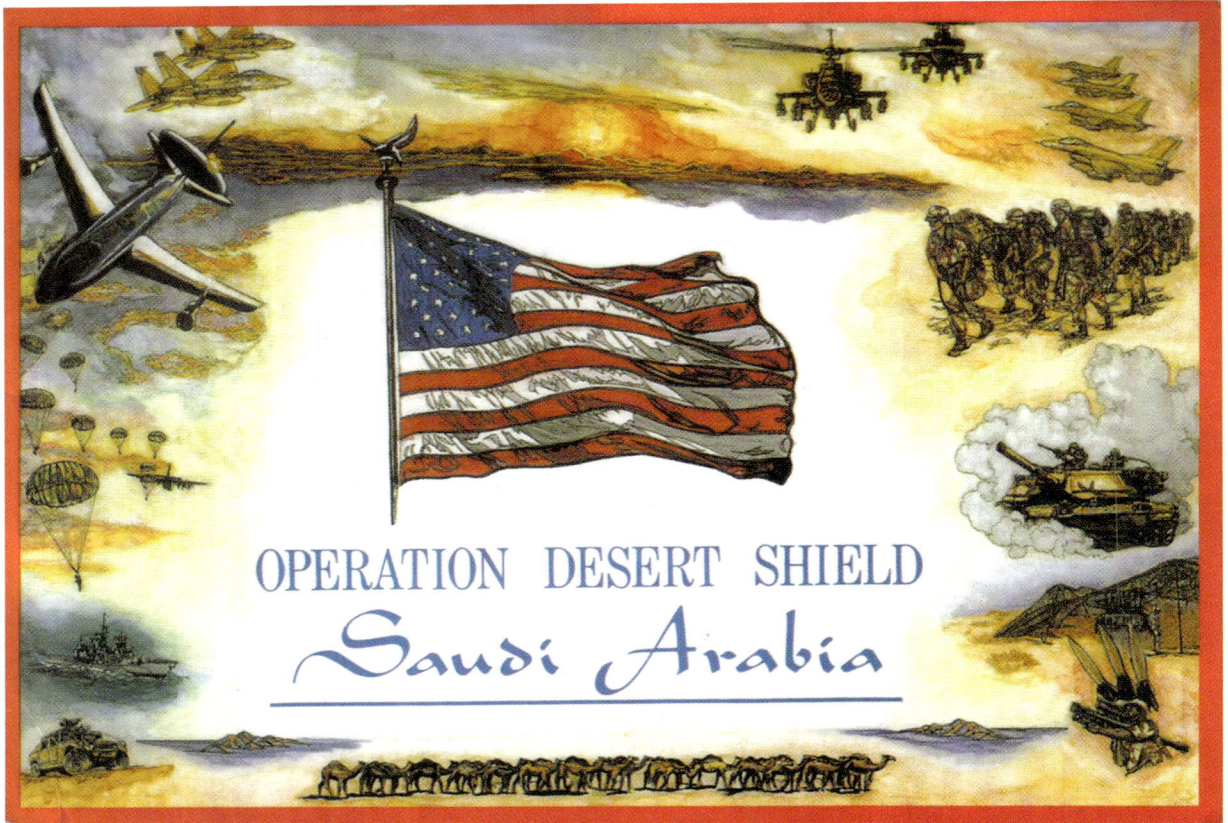

OPERATION DESERT SHIELD
Saudi Arabia

Operation Desert Shield was instigated following Saddam Hussein's invasion of Kuwait on 2 August 1990.

The man put in charge of the international effort to protect Saudi Arabia was General H. Norman Schwarzkopf, Commander of US Central Command or CENTCOM.

F-15E Eagles of USAF's 4th Tactical Fighter Wing, consisting of the 335th and 336th Tactical Fighter Squadrons, gathered at Al Kharj, Saudi Arabia. Such congestion caused General Schwarzkopf great concern: if an Iraqi aircraft had got through the air defences, it could have caused havoc.

Amongst the aircraft deployed to Saudi Arabia were two squadrons of the highly distinctive F-117A Night Hawk stealth attack aircraft, which were based at Khamis Mushait Air Force Base from August 1990 to March 1991. These aircraft were given the task of destroying Saddam Hussein's command and control structures, as well as his WMD facilities prior to the ground war.

The RAF deployed both the Tornado F3 air superiority fighter and the Tornado GR1 long-range interdictor to Dhahran, Muharraq and Tabuk. This particular GR1 is from 15 Squadron, which operated from Muharraq.

Low-level air defence for British forces was provided by the British Aerospace Rapier surface-to-air missile system. Initially Saddam's powerful air force and arsenal of ballistic missiles posed a serious threat to the gathering coalition forces.

US ground forces were supported by almost 2,000 M1A1 Abrams tanks. These particular examples are undergoing testing at the US Lima tank plant. The US Marine Corps also deployed several hundred M60 tanks to the Gulf.

The M1 Abrams entered US Army service in 1980. Resources in 1991 consisted of the M1 and the upgraded M1A1, neither of which had seen combat before Desert Storm.

The British Army called on forces stationed in Germany as part of the British Army of the Rhine. Amongst them was the 7th Armoured Brigade, based at Fallingbostel.

British armour deployed to the Gulf included the Challenger 1 tank, which went into service in the mid-1980s. Like the American Abrams, it was not battle-tested.

The Royal Artillery's field regiments were equipped with US-made M109A2 self-propelled howitzers. M109 variants were employed by most of the armed forces serving with the Coalition.

A major concern was Saddam Hussein's weapons of mass destruction, in particular his chemical weapons. As a result, British troops deployed to the Gulf with their nuclear, biological and chemical (NBC) equipment. They were issued with the No. 1 Mk 4 NBC protective suit in disruptive pattern camouflage scheme (seen here), the S10 respirator, butyl rubber gloves and Mk 4 boots.

This vital piece of kit is a British Warrior Mechanized Combat Repair Vehicle (MCRV), pictured in Saudi Arabia serving with the British 7th Armoured Brigade, 1st Armoured Division. Such vehicles were indispensable in keeping an armoured division on the move.

A similar Warrior Mechanized Recovery Vehicle. Note the raised earth anchor at the rear; this is lowered to stabilize the vehicle before deploying the hydraulically operated crane.

France's AMX-30 main battle tank armed with a 120mm gun was used by the French, Saudis and Qataris during the operations conducted in 1991. Saudi Arabia had 290 AMX-30s and Qatar 24. This example belongs to the French 6th Light Armoured Division supporting Desert Storm.

The Coalition's ability to drive Saddam from Kuwait was no foregone conclusion. Here (*left to right*) General Colin Powell, Chairman US Joint Chiefs of Staff, CENTCOM CinC General Schwarzkopf and Under-Secretary of Defense Paul D. Wolfowitz look rather pensive as they listen to a briefing by the US Secretary of Defense Dick Cheney.

All coalition members took the threat of Iraqi chemical weapons very seriously. This Syrian is taking part in a chemical and biological warfare exercise just before the ground war to liberate Kuwait commenced. He is armed with the Chinese Type 56-I assault rifle.

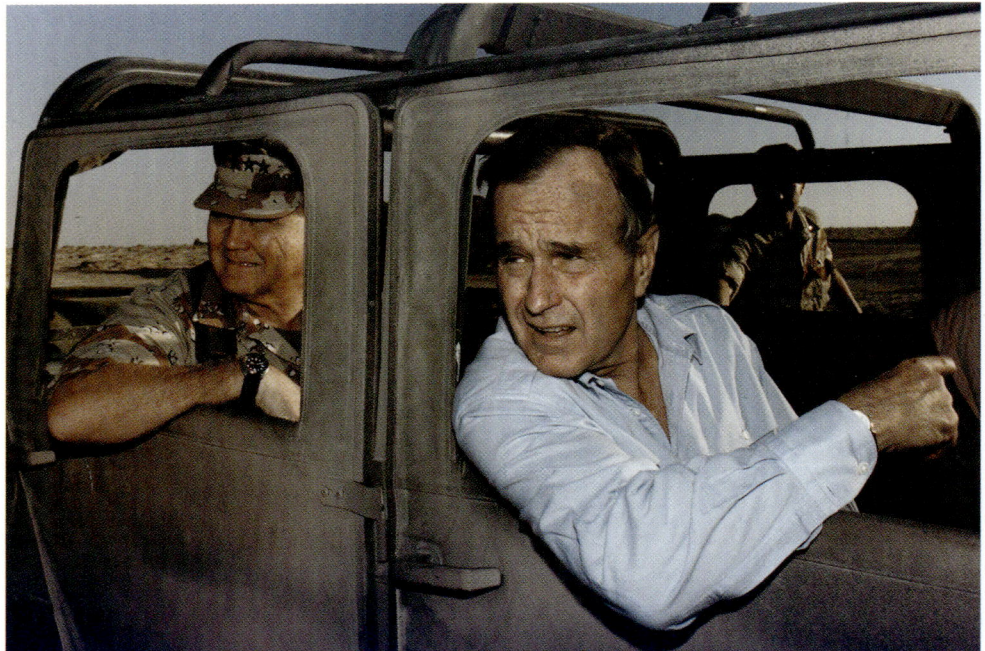

President Bush and General Schwarzkopf pictured during a tour of their forces in Saudi Arabia.

Chapter Two

Saddam in the KTO

By early January 1991 western intelligence reports suggested that Saddam's forces deployed in the Kuwaiti Theatre of Operations (KTO), encompassing Kuwait and southern Iraq, numbered approximately 540,000 men, equipped with 4,000 tanks, 2,700 armoured personnel carriers (APCs) and other armoured fighting vehicles (AFVs), and 3,000 pieces of artillery. This force included the 120,000–150,000-strong elite Republican Guard Corps. These figures were based on the assessment that forty-three Iraqi divisions were in the KTO. On the face of it, this was a formidable fighting force that would not be easy to defeat.

To make matter worse, overall Saddam Hussein had almost a million men under arms, consisting of seven corps directing seven armoured/mechanized divisions plus forty-two infantry divisions, whilst the Republican Guard had four armoured/mechanized divisions and three infantry divisions. Despite its huge manpower and powerful armoured forces, closer inspection showed that the Iraqi Army's fearsome reputation was based largely on myth. Its military reputation was not as great as it had been made out to be, and certainly its track record during the Iran–Iraq War was nothing to boast about. The Iraqi Army had not conquered great swathes of Iran and it had struggled to fight Iran's massed human-wave attacks to a bloody standstill.

The Iraqis had considerable but somewhat mixed experiences of armoured warfare. In 1973 the Iraqi 3rd Armoured Division had been committed in support of the Syrians, but performed fairly poorly, losing 140 tanks to the Israelis. This was followed by nine years of war with Iran between 1980 and 1989. However, tactical use of tanks on both sides was at best unimaginative. There had been no grand blitzkriegs across Iran or Iraq. Nonetheless, within the Iraqi armed forces Saddam's Republican Guard Corps had gained a particularly tough reputation. While hardly comparable to Hitler's Waffen-SS, during the Iran–Iraq conflict the Republican Guard had formed a strategic reserve, acting as a 'fire-brigade' that was sent to any front that was in need of bolstering. It fought on almost every front and in most of the major battles, expanding from a single armoured brigade in 1980 to one infantry, one commando and three armoured brigades by 1987. Four years later it was claimed that the corps consisted of seven whole divisions. Whenever the Republican Guard appeared, Iraqi morale was greatly improved, as was their combat performance. These observations were not lost on western planners.

Principal Iraqi Armoured units in the KTO:
Republican Guard Corps:
Hammurabi, Medina and Tawakalna Armoured Divisions

Iraqi Army:
3rd, 6th, 10th, 12th, 17th and 37th Armoured Divisions
1st, 5th, 14th and 51st Mechanized Divisions
26th Armoured Brigade
20th Mechanized Brigade

Despite the impressive numbers, the truth was that neither the Iraqi Army nor the Republican Guard had been given time to recover from the gruelling conflict with Iran. In 1990 Iraq was still equipped with the Brazilian, Chinese, Czech and Russian armour with which it had fought the Iran–Iraq War. Much of it was poorly serviced and in desperate need of spares. Saddam's armoured forces were equipped with some 5,500 tanks comprising 2,500 Russian T-54/55s, 1,500 Chinese Type 59/69s, 1,000 Russian T-62s and 500 T-72s, as well as 8,100 APCs consisting of Russian BMP-1/2 Infantry Fighting Vehicles, BTR-50/60/152 and MTLBs, Czech OT-62/63s, Chinese YW-531s, American M113s and Brazilian EE-11s. These were supported by no fewer than 500 Russian-supplied self-propelled guns of 122mm, 152mm and 155mm calibre, and 3,200 pieces of artillery and multiple rocket launchers.

The bulk of the Iraqi tank fleet consisted of the tried and tested Soviet-supplied T-54/55, T-62 and T-72 types, all of which were decidedly long in the tooth by 1990. The T-72 was the Iraqi Army's most modern tank during Desert Storm, although it was a good ten years older than the US Abrams. A few Iraqi-upgraded Russian T-54/55s and Chinese Type-59/69 tanks with additional frontal arc armour (giving a greater degree of protection against high-explosive anti-tank rounds) were encountered by coalition tanks during the fighting. Some of the Iraqi T-62s were also modified in a number of areas (including the addition of covers to the turret-mounted searchlights). It was not known if any had been modified to fire laser-guided missiles via the 115mm gun. Egypt also supplied Iraq with 140 M-77s, a Romanian copy of the T-54 that was also known as the M1977 or TR-77.

The Americans had very good intelligence on the T-55/62 and even the T-72, in part due to the Arab–Israeli wars. The Israelis first fought the T-54/55 in 1967 and the T-62 in 1973. During the 1967 Six-Day War the Arabs lost 1,072 tanks and about another 2,000 in the 1973 Yom Kippur War, and many were passed on to the US for exploitation. The guns of both types performed poorly in long-range exchanges (over 1,500m), and while the T-62's 115mm U5-T smoothbore gun was effective, crew performance was hampered by cramped conditions. Likewise their excellent armour was compromised by the location of internal fuel and ammunition stores (adding greatly to the risk of internal detonation, even by a glancing hit). The Soviet-designed tanks also had a tendency to overheat in the desert, thereby aggravating the already severe problems of crew discomfort.

Combat experience had already shown that the 105mm/M68 tank gun firing armour-piercing fin-stabilized discarding sabot (APFSDS) projectiles was capable of penetrating the frontal armour of early T-72s. The Abrams' 120mm gun had the added advantage of firing the M829 APFSDS-T (T - tracer) round with a depleted uranium penetrator. This meant that the M1A1 Abrams and the 105mm-armed M60 could easily deal with the cream of the Iraqi armour. In fact the US Department of Defense was almost ecstatic over the Abrams' performance in the Gulf. Likewise the British Challenger's 120mm weapon could knock out enemy tanks at 2,500 yards and beyond, and with its excellent thermal sights it was just as effective at night. Its Chobham armour was also enhanced by the addition of extra armour packs on the front and sides.

The Soviet-designed 2S1 self-propelled howitzer entered service in the early 1970s and remained in production until around 1991. Iraq is believed to have imported about 140 of these and the 2S3 in the late 1980s, and several were subsequently captured during Desert Storm. The 2S3 self-propelled howitzer had also entered Soviet service in the early 1970s and some 10,000 examples of this type were built. Numbers of Iraqi 2S3s were overrun in 1991, their crews probably having fled in the face of overwhelming air attacks.

In 1989 the Iraqis displayed a BMP-1 Infantry Combat Vehicle with appliqué armour fitted to the sides of the hull for protection against 12.7mm and 14.5mm armour-piercing rounds. However, none was fitted to the turret or glacis plate. Holes were also cut into the hull armour package to allow the infantry to use their small arms from within the vehicle. It is not known whether this type entered service with the Iraqi Army in quantity. The Iraqis obtained a small number of BMD-1 Airborne Combat Vehicles, and a number in poor condition were later captured in Kuwait. They were presumably used in a fire support or reconnaissance role.

The Soviet-built MT-LB Multi-purpose Tracked Vehicle was used as an artillery tractor for 100mm and 122mm guns, as a command vehicle, as an artillery fire control vehicle, as a cargo carrier and as an APC. Iraq is believed to have imported up to 800 of them during the 1980s, and some were modified to carry an Egyptian-supplied 120mm mortar. Many of the MT-LBs came from Bulgaria, which built them under licence.

Iraq had acquired about 300 EE-9 Cascavel fast and well-armed Brazilian 6x6 armoured cars during the 1980s. A number were deployed with the Iraqi garrison in Kuwait City in 1990 and were subsequently caught by air strikes trying to flee north. The Iraqis also imported several hundred Brazilian EE-3 Jararaca scout cars and EE-11 Urutu 6x6 APCs.

The OT-62 Armoured Personnel Carrier jointly developed by Czechoslovakia and Poland in the 1960s was largely a copy of the Soviet BTR-50. Iraq procured about 500 of these and the wheeled OT-64. The OT-64 Armoured Personnel Carrier 8x8 wheeled APC served the same function as the Soviet BTR-60 APC (although they are not physically the same). Production ceased in 1990, by which time 10,300 had been built for home and export markets.

The Chinese Type YW-531 tracked APC was developed in the late 1960s and saw combat in Angola, Iraq, Kuwait, Tanzania and Vietnam. From 1983 onwards Iraq received some 500 of these vehicles, a number of which were captured in 1991, including the Type YW-701 command post vehicle (based on the YW-531 and deployed by regimental and divisional commanders) and several Type YW-750 ambulances. This APC would first see action with the Iraqi Army at Khafji in Saudi Arabia.

All in all, Saddam's forces in the KTO were not to be underestimated, and while western intelligence had a good idea how they might perform, it was certainly far from a foregone conclusion. Saddam and his generals were gambling on being able to inflict sufficient casualties on the coalition forces to compel the coalition commanders to accept a ceasefire brokered by the UN Security Council. The reality was that Saddam's timing could not have been worse, especially as his key ally, the Soviet Union, was in the throes of disintegration and was in no position to influence events. Nor was it able to offer a massive re-supply operation as it had done with Egypt and Syria during the Arab–Israeli Wars. Saddam was on his own.

If there was one thing Saddam had a lot of, it was tanks and other armoured vehicles. This is an Iraqi M-1974 (2S1) 122mm self-propelled gun supplied by the Soviet Union.

The Iraqis were also equipped with the Soviet M-1973 (2S3) 152mm self-propelled howitzer, which, along with the 2S1, formed the divisional artillery of their armoured units.

Brazil also supplied Saddam with armour. This is an Iraqi ENGESA EE-9 Cascavel armoured car sporting an interesting camouflage scheme and armed with a Giat Industries 90mm gun. Saddam acquired about 250 of these vehicles.

Iraq first took delivery of the Chinese NORINCO Type 69 main battle tank armed with a 100mm gun in 1983, while at war with Iran. This example is a Type 69-II with the laser range-finder over the main armament.

Another Chinese-supplied Type 69-II. In total, it is thought Saddam received around 400 of these and the earlier Type 59, both of which were derived from the Soviet T-54.

A Polish-built T-55 upgraded by the Iraqis with additional frontal armour designed to protect it from HEAT rounds. The Iraqis also upgraded some of their Chinese Type 59/69 tanks. This example belonged to the Iraqi 5th Mechanized Division and is now preserved at the Tank Museum.

Saddam also had a considerable stock of Scud ballistic missiles. These are Scud Bs, modified by the Iraqis.

This Iraqi ZIL-135 carrying a FROG-7 short-range artillery rocket was captured by the US Marines. Iraq also built its own variant, known as the Laith 90, along with chemical warheads for the FROG rocket.

An Mi-24 Helicopter gunship belonging to the Iraqi Army Air Corps. By the late 1980s Iraq had about forty of these helicopters, which were used extensively during the Iran–Iraq War.

(*Above*) An Iraqi Bell 214 ST transport helicopter. The Iraqi Air Force had a fairly large transport fleet. These helicopters were instrumental in helping to crush the rising after Operation Desert Sabre.

(*Opposite, top*) During the build-up to Desert Storm/Desert Sabre, Saddam harassed both Saudi Arabia and Israel with FROG and Scud attacks. The Scud's inaccuracy meant that it was not a viable military weapon, so Saddam resorted to using it as a terror weapon against civilian targets.

(*Opposite, bottom*) This Iraqi Scud was intercepted by a US Patriot air defence missile over Saudi Arabia. In total Saddam launched eighty-six Scuds, forty of them against Israel and the remainder against Saudi Arabia. Israel, though, refused to be provoked into widening the war.

Iraqi generals watching a female militia member field-stripping a Romanian Kalashnikov assault rifle.

A Yugoslavian-built M-84 tank delivered in Saudi Arabia for use by the Free Kuwaiti forces. Ordered prior to Saddam's invasion, the M-84 was an upgraded version of the Soviet T-72M used by the Iraqis.

Chapter Three

Desert Storm

Once the coalition air forces began to build up in Saudi Arabia for Operation Desert Shield, the bulk of the Iraqi Air Force's combat aircraft were withdrawn from their southern bases to sites well north of Baghdad. This meant that only surface-to-air missiles (SAMs) and anti-aircraft artillery (AAA) defended the southern bases. In preparation for the liberation of Kuwait General Schwarzkopf planned to target forty-four Iraqi airfields, some sixteen of them primary airfields and the remainder dispersal fields.

Saddam's pre-Desert Storm confidence was founded largely on his faith in the survivability of his air force; after all, it had resolutely withstood eight years of war with Iran. Indeed, the Iraqi Air Force's (IrAF) vast infrastructure was primarily designed to protect against pre-emptive attack, with its absolutely huge airfields and concrete hardened aircraft shelters (HAS).

While Saddam was able to deploy massive ground forces, he also had a sizeable and modern air and air defence system. At the time debate raged about the exact composition of the Iraqi Air Force. Even the British intelligence community did not have a comprehensive ORBAT, despite the focus and implications of the Iran–Iraq War. RAF Tornado pilot Flight Lieutenant John Peters recalled, 'The worst case intelligence assessments were that the Iraqis had over 700 combat aircraft, excluding helicopters.' Their most potent aircraft were almost 50 MiG-29s, 70 F-1s, 30 MiG-25s and, according to Peters, 'whole swarms' of MiG-23s, Su-22s and Su-25s. On paper the IrAF looked formidable but, despite its material strength, its pilots were judged to be poor, serviceability was low and it was ineffective in the close air support (CAS) role. It was also notable that IrAF training levels between August 1990 and January 1991 were almost non-existent.

To coalition intelligence the clear weakness in the Iraqi military structure was the complete lack of air support. General Schwarzkopf also highlighted Iraq's 'feeble logistics' and the 'centralized system of command and control in which important decisions even in the heat of the battle, could only be taken by Saddam personally'. Furthermore, the IrAF was fielding at least fifteen types of fixed-wing combat aircraft and sixteen types of helicopter. Ten of its MiG-29s were two-seaters with no radar, severely limiting their combat value. Nor did the IrAF have any all-weather capability: during the Iran–Iraq War it had been restricted even by low cloud and rain.

By 1991 the IrAF had up to 750 fighters and ground-attack aircraft in its formidable inventory. On top of this, the Iraqi Army Air Corps (IAAC) fielded about 150 combat helicopters. Similarly Iraq's Air Defence Command was armed with 7,000 surface-to-air missiles and 6,000 anti-aircraft artillery pieces directed by a national radar network. The Republican Guard had its own system to defend key sites such as Baghdad, with 60 SAM batteries and 3,000 AAA guns.

In reality, though, probably fewer than ninety of the IrAF's 113 French-supplied F-1s and only half of its fifty Russian MiG-29s were operable, while about 100 of its 200 MiG-21/F-7s remained. When the Desert Storm air war came to a close in early March 1991, Iraq had as few as a hundred fighters left from its once mighty order of battle.

In total, the IrAF had some fifty-four bases, consisting of twenty-four main operating bases and another thirty dispersal fields. Some of these were colossal: up to twice the size of Heathrow airport. They were protected by a reasonably well-integrated air defence system and scattered across them were 594 hardened aircraft shelters.

Since its creation, arms deliveries to the IrAF had been substantial; for example, in the 1960s they were three times as great as in the previous decade. Up until 1955 the Iraqi forces were under British military auspices, but even after that date the IrAF continued to receive British aircraft such as the Vampire and Venom (the US also provided a handful of Sabres). The ousting of the Iraqi monarchy in 1958 saw Baghdad turn to Moscow, and in November 1958 the IrAF began to take delivery of its first Soviet aircraft, which included MiG-17s, Yak-11s and Il-28s. The following year the RAF withdrew from Habbaniyah and the USSR provided Iraq with MiG-17Ds, Tu-16s and An-12s. The Soviet Union's vast armament factories were to deluge Baghdad with aircraft over the next two decades.

The expansion of the IrAF from 1961 to 1970 was driven in part by the need to counter the Kurdish guerrillas fighting for autonomy in the north of the country. The IrAF successfully deployed Jet Provosts and Il-28s against the Kurds. In 1964 the IrAF ordered British Hunters and Jet Provosts, but Baghdad began to drift back into the Soviet sphere as it sought fighters and trainers on a scale and on credit terms Britain could never match. After the 1972 Soviet–Iraqi Treaty of Friendship and Co-operation Moscow provided the backbone of the IrAF, including MiG-21s, MiG-23s, Su-7s, Su-20s, Tu-22s and Il-28s. The IrAF's need for more aircraft and ordnance was fuelled by a renewal of the Kurdish insurgency in the mid-1970s and the USSR provided further MiG-23s as well as MiG-27s.

During the mid-1980s the IrAF also received a steady stream of equipment from other countries, including Argentinian Pucaras, Brazilian Tucanos, Chinese F-7s, French Mirage F-1s and Italian AB-212 and A-109 helicopters. Russia also furnished Baghdad with MiG-23/25/29 fighter aircraft and Mi-24 helicopter gunships. Deliveries of highly sophisticated aircraft and missiles enabled Iraq to expand the strategic scope of its war against Iran.

Iraq's chemical weapons were a cause for concern, particularly when activity at various air bases during the latter half of 1990 may have included the positioning of chemical weapons in ordnance bunkers ready for deployment. Luckily a planned Tu-16 chemical bombing raid never came to fruition.

Baghdad's use of chemical weapons against Iran and its own Kurds has been well documented. Notably, during the Iran–Iraq War the IrAF provided the only means of delivery beyond artillery range. It conducted missions using 250 and 500-gauge bombs filled with chemical agents dropped from Soviet-supplied Su-17 and MiG-23 jets. The IrAF's complicity in Baghdad's Weapons of Mass Destruction programmes was inescapable.

In the meantime Saddam and his commanders had virtually no intelligence on their opponents' air forces, except perhaps the overwhelming numbers facing them. However, the IrAF did have one intelligence coup. On 11 November 1990 a Saudi Air Force F-15 defected to Sudan. America and Saudi Arabia demanded the immediate return of the aircraft, but it remained in Sudan for several days. During that time Iraqi intelligence may have had the opportunity to examine the F-15 and it is believed that they interrogated the pilot. The IrAF could have gained valuable information on Saudi tactical frequencies, electronic warning, electronic counter-measures and communications.

The Coalition's combined air forces launched Desert Storm in mid-January 1991, targeting Saddam's command and control sites, Scud missile installations and lines of communication around the clock. On the face of it the coalition air forces had their work cut out. Whilst Iraq's air defences were considerable, Flight Lieutenant Peters and his RAF colleagues were also conscious of the threat from small arms. Peters observed, 'Since it takes very little wit to fire a gun into the air, Saddam Hussein's threat of creating "lead walls" – curtains of fire for us happy chappies to fly into – had to be taken seriously.' Nevertheless, the vital air superiority over Kuwait and Iraq was achieved within just twenty-four hours of the first air attacks. The Iraqi Air Force was shot out of the sky, destroyed on the ground or fled. It lost almost 50 per cent of its holdings: 141 aircraft were claimed destroyed on the ground and a further 35 in air-to-air engagements, whilst 122 fled to Iran, never to be returned. The national air defence system was quickly and efficiently smashed to pieces.

Over a six-week period the coalition air forces also focused on the Republican Guard's tanks and other armoured vehicles. Approximately 35,000 sorties were launched against Iraqi ground forces, of which 5,600 were directed at the Guard, dug in over a 4,000 square mile area. Initial estimates of Iraqi losses to air strikes were about 40 Republican Guard tanks, whilst the army lost 52 tanks, 55 artillery pieces and 178 trucks. According to CENTCOM, Iraqi execution battalions patrolled the front-line units, shooting deserters or anyone listening to coalition media.

The tempo of the coalition air campaign against Saddam was quite astonishing. No fewer than 109,500 combat sorties were flown, mostly by the Americans, dropping 88,500 tons of munitions. The Americans also committed to action sixty-two venerable B-52 bombers; these veterans of the Vietnam War flew 1,600 sorties and accounted for 30 per cent of the tonnage dropped.

General Schwarzkopf wanted a 50 per cent degradation of Iraqi fighting capabilities by the air campaign before committing himself to the ground war. Assuming that the estimates of the Iraqi forces in the KTO were correct, they more than achieved this. Just before the ground offensive the Coalition claimed the destruction of up to 1,300 Iraqi tanks, 800 armoured personnel carriers and 1,100 artillery pieces. Instead of withdrawing, Saddam announced he would fight the 'Mother of battles'. The scene was set for the inevitable ground war.

These Free Kuwaiti McDonnell-Douglas A-4KU Skyhawks managed to escape Saddam's clutches. Initially their pilots were denied weapons for fear they might start the war before the Coalition was ready. The aircraft are seen here being fuelled up prior to a mission on 13 February 1991.

The business end of the RAF's Tornado. These fighters operated from Dhahran, Muharraq and Tabuk Air Bases in Saudi Arabia, with about fifty Tornados deployed to the Gulf. The yellow missiles are Air-Launched Anti-Radiation Missiles (ALARMs), designed to destroy enemy radars. A total of 121 ALARMs were fired in 1991. The Iraqi Army had no real answer to such ordnance.

A Panavia Tornado F3 air superiority fighter carrying two AIM-9 Sidewinder and four Skyflash air-to-air missiles. There were some air-to-air engagements with the Iraqi Air Force but not many.

The F-117A Stealth fighters of the 37th Tactical Fighter Wing played a key role in the Coalition's air war against Iraq. They were tasked to attack Iraqi weapons of mass destruction sites and command and control facilities.

The USAF committed a variety of aircraft to Desert Storm, including the American Fairchild Republic A-10A Thunderbolt. Armed with the nose-mounted 30mm GAU-8/A Avenger rotary cannon, it was a devastating battlefield weapon. It also carried Maverick air-to-surface missiles, unguided rockets and cluster bombs. These aircraft were instrumental in helping thwart Saddam's armoured attack at Khafji.

Under Operation Friction, Canada deployed three squadrons of Canadian Armed Forces McDonnell-Douglas CF-18 Hornet fighters to Doha in Qatar. Their main role was to protect Canadian warships in the Gulf.

The RAF's rather ancient BAe Buccaneer S2b was called upon to provide target laser illumination for laser-guided bombs launched by other aircraft.

The Iraqis' hardened shelters offered their aircraft no protection against coalition ordnance. Here a US Navy F-14 Tomcat flies over a smashed concrete shelter on an Iraqi air base. It could be argued that coalition air power won the war. Laser-guided bombs were so accurate that coalition aircraft could put two bombs into the same crater.

The melted and scorched remains of an Iraqi Su-25 Frogfoot ground-attack aircraft destroyed at Jalibah air base on 3 March 1991.

One of the Iraqi Air Force's more capable aircraft was the Mikoyan-Gurevich MiG-29 Fulcrum; this one was hit with pinpoint precision during Desert Storm. This aircraft has also been identified as the earlier MiG-25 Foxbat. USAF McDonnell-Douglas F-15C Eagle fighters shot down at least five Iraqi MiG-29s.

These concrete hardened aircraft shelters at Ahmed Al Jaber were penetrated by bunker-busting bombs. This photograph was taken by an F-14 Tomcat using the Tactical Air Reconnaissance Pod System (TARPS). In total the coalition air forces flew 109,876 sorties; the US air and naval forces expended 6,520 tons of precision-guided munitions alone.

Desert Storm also targeted the Iraqi Army and Republican Guard, as this burnt-out Iraqi T-54A or Type 59 tank testifies. Sand berms screened the tank's hull from enemy armour but did little to protect it from air attack.

A close-up of the burnt tail section of an Iraqi Phantom II aircraft destroyed on the ground by Allied air attacks during Operation Desert Storm.

The coalition air forces did not have it all their own way. The Iraqis managed to bring down this F-16C from the 614th Tactical Fighter Squadron, ironically known as the 'Lucky Devils.'

Chapter Four

Saddam's Fist

Following Saddam Hussein's invasion of Kuwait, he optimistically decided to pre-empt the impending ground war in the hope of provoking the Coalition before it was ready. If he seized the initiative and generated enough momentum, he reasoned, he could suck in the coalition forces piecemeal, inflict casualties and secure prisoners, thereby damaging coalition morale and unity in the glare of the world's media.

Although it was anticipated that the fighting would take place largely in the deserts of Saudi Arabia and Iraq, there was concern that a major urban battle would have to be fought to liberate Kuwait City. A taste of potential things to come occurred on 30 January 1991 when an unexpected urban engagement was fought in the Saudi town of Khafji.

Kuwait's large Wafra oilfield straddles the Kuwaiti–Saudi border and lies just to the west of the Kuwaiti town of Wafra. The nearest Saudi town is Khafji, which lies on the coast to the south-east about 20km from the Kuwaiti border. The Wafra oilfield is in a so-called neutral oil zone shared by Kuwait and Saudi Arabia, and was jointly operated by the Kuwait Oil Company and the American oil giant Texaco. Saudi Arabia and Kuwait shared the production. One of Saddam's reasons for invading his neighbour was that the Kuwaitis were pumping out such large quantities of oil that it was forcing down global oil prices. This in turn was affecting Iraqi oil revenues at time when Saddam was trying to replenish his country's coffers following the disastrous Iran–Iraq war.

Khafji first came to notice on 16 January 1991 when an oil storage tank was struck by Iraqi shelling. The town formed the only junction on the coastal road linking Saudi Arabia with Kuwait to the north and Bahrain, Qatar, the UAE and Oman to the south. Saddam's artillery, sited beyond the Kuwaiti border, heralded his campaign of environmental vandalism, during which he wrecked Kuwait's oilfields. The shelling caused a major fire and a billowing cloud of black smoke lingered over the town like some ominous storm warning.

As Khafji was well within Iraqi artillery range, coalition forces were obliged to remain far to the south, in effect leaving the town undefended. In light of the danger, the town's population of some 15,000 people was quickly evacuated. The whole world knew that Khafji had been empty for two weeks after global news networks broadcast scenes of the dust-blown empty streets. It was a vacuum that Saddam intended to fill. As it had been evacuated, there was no risk of civilian casualties, but unfortunately for the Iraqis the town was open plan, with mainly two-storey buildings. Therefore rather than providing a defender's paradise, it actually gave them nowhere to hide.

In hindsight it seems a foolhardy operation, but at the time it presented a good opportunity to Saddam. The town was close to Iraqi defensive forces within the KTO that could provide cover; it was within easy reach of the Iraqi Air Force and, being on the coast, the Iraqi Navy could also intervene. Furthermore the area was defended largely by Saudi forces, which Saddam may have felt would be a soft option. The neighbouring US Marines were also to be drawn into the town and pinned down by a frontal attack. A flanking Iraqi tank force was then to strike them from the west, whilst to the east troops were to be landed by the Iraqi Navy. Saddam planned to make a total of four forays along the border from Wafra eastward to Khafji on the coast.

Just across the Kuwaiti border Saddam's spearhead for the Khafji attack consisted of the elite 5th Mechanized Division. (In organizational terms, Iraqi mechanized divisions had two mechanized brigades and one armoured brigade, while armoured divisions had two armoured brigades and one mechanized brigade. Armoured brigades had three armoured battalions and one mechanized battalion, while mechanized brigades had three mechanized battalions and a tank battalion.) The 5th Division's parent corps planned to launch a simultaneous four-pronged assault. It is unclear if it was part of a wider attack down the Wadi al-Batin, though the lack of adequate air cover made this unlikely. However, to reinforce the attack on Khafji three other mechanized divisions, comprising some 60,000 men and 240 tanks, were gathered near Wafra in Kuwait. It is notable that the elite Republican Guard was not assigned any part in this operation. The other key player, the Iraqi Air Force, was also conspicuous by its complete absence.

It was the Saudis who would bear the brunt of Saddam's assault at Khafji. Six days after the bombardment began, Iraqi armoured forces were detected deploying a convoy towards Saudi Arabia. The coalition response was swift and an air strike destroyed fifty-six vehicles. Normally, once a hit was scored, the Iraqi crews of any neighbouring vehicles would abandon their equipment and run, leaving them to be picked off.

Leading elements of the Iraqi 5th Mechanized Division, up to brigade strength (three or four battalions), comprising some 2,000 men with fifty T-54/55 main battle tanks and BMP/YW 531 tracked APCs, moved out over a 50-mile front on the night of 29 January. They crossed the Kuwaiti border undetected and pushed south, supported by seventeen fast patrol boats, which moved down the coast bearing commando landing parties.

The RAF pounced on the naval element of the assault, hitting at least two of the vessels and scattering the others. The Royal Navy also attacked Iraqi patrol boats that may have been intended for the Khafji operation on 29 January 1991, when the British frigate HMS *Gloucester* launched Lynx helicopters armed with Sea Skua missiles. A second convoy appeared the following day, including an Iraqi minesweeper, three fast attack boats and three landing ships. RAF Jaguar and USAF A-6 jets attacked them. In the desperate Battle of Bubiyan Island twenty Iraqi naval craft attempted to flee to Iranian waters. Chase was given and only two damaged vessels survived the aerial onslaught; the rest were left blazing wrecks.

In the face of Saddam's incursion, the Coalition's first move was to cut his lines of communication between Kuwait and Khafji. British RAF Jaguar jets and American A-10 Thunderbolt tank-busting aircraft were despatched to attack any forces north of the town. American Marine Corps Cobra attack helicopters and 155mm artillery were also used to seal off the town.

About 90km from the coast a supporting Iraqi tank brigade ran into the US 1st Marine Division's light armored infantry battalion. The firefight that followed involved American attack helicopters and A-10s, and Saddam's forces lost twenty-four tanks and thirteen other vehicles. An Iraqi tank managed to account for a single Marine Light Armoured Vehicle (LAV), whilst a second was inadvertently destroyed by friendly fire. The Americans suffered eleven dead, seven of them in the friendly fire incident. This resulted in aerial recognition signs being added to every coalition vehicle, with inverted white Vs being painted on the sides and an orange marker on the top.

A second supporting Iraqi brigade bounced off the US 2nd Marine Division's Light Armored Infantry Battalion. One LAV with tube-launched, optically tracked, wire-guided (TOW) missiles accounted for two Iraqi tanks. To the west of the town the Iraqi 15th Mechanized Regiment ran into a Qatari tank unit. All these Iraqi forces also suffered air attacks and fell back, losing eighty vehicles outside Khafji. Remarkably, the Iraqis' other armoured battalion, however, was to push aside a screening Saudi force and occupy Khafji.

Late on 29 January, or early on the 30th, the Saudis heard that fifty-seven Iraqi armoured vehicles were heading towards Khafji's desalination plant. A company of lightly armed Saudi Marines was quickly withdrawn from the town. The initial slowness of coalition air forces to respond to this threat was due to the American Marines struggling to turn back elements of the 20th Mechanized Brigade and 26th Armoured Brigade further west.

A dozen Kuwaiti soldiers were occupying a bunker in the middle of the town, from where they had been reporting on oil slicks. The BBC correspondent David Shukman scathingly reported, 'Just as Kuwaiti troops saw no point in putting up a fight when their country was invaded, so they judged it useless to resist on the moonlight night of 29 January when Iraqi tanks rolled forward into Khafji. Following the example set by their emir on 2 August [1990], the Kuwaitis jumped into their private cars, which were parked next to the bunker, and fled for their lives.'

'The Iraqi attack came as a surprise,' recalled Alan Munro, Britain's Ambassador to Saudi Arabia at the time. 'Indeed, the press first came to hear of it when a correspondent tried to call the town's hotel and found an Iraqi soldier answering the call.'

During the early hours a flight of Cobra helicopters from the US 369th Gunfighter Wing hunted down Iraqi armour using night-vision goggles but had to return to base when they ran low on fuel. They were replaced by four more Cobras, which destroyed a platoon-sized mechanized force. By about 5.00am the Saudis had realized that Saddam really meant business, as about twelve Iraqi armoured vehicles were observed on the western edge of the town. Nevertheless, no Iraqi tanks entered Khafji; they had all been knocked out to the north, although some armoured fighting vehicles did get in.

Initially the Saudi commander, Prince Khalid Bin Sultan al-Saud, panicked, because it had been his decision to remove the Khafji garrison. It also seems he may not have informed his uncle King Fahd, who was understandably furious that Saddam was now occupying part of his kingdom. General Schwarzkopf was horrified when he was informed that King Fahd wanted Khafji flattened by American bombers. 'I am sorry,' responded Schwarzkopf, 'we don't conduct ourselves that way. Can you imagine how it would look in the eyes of the world if the United States of America bombed a Saudi town into rubble just because a few Iraqis were there?'

The following day, under a relentless assault from A-10s, the other two attacking Iraqi battalions failed to get through. Inside Khafji, although a brigade of 2,000 men had been thrown into the attack, the Iraqis only numbered about 600 defenders with infantry support weapons and some tanks on the outskirts. This solitary battalion, acting as Saddam's fist in Saudi Arabia, was to hold out bravely for two days. Although the town had no real military value, the Coalition could not leave it. Aside from the inevitable loss of face, two US Marine reconnaissance parties were trapped in Khafji along with the Iraqi soldiers.

US Secretary of Defense Richard Cheney pictured in conference with Crown Prince Abdullah, who was also in charge of the Saudi National Guard. It fell to this force to liberate the Saudi town of Khafji after it was occupied by the Iraqi Army.

A Tornado F3 of the Royal Saudi Air Force in January 1991. The Saudis had three squadrons of Tornados, plus one in the process of forming, all based at Dhahran.

Armour of the Royal Saudi Land Forces' 20th Brigade, comprising French-supplied AMX-10P infantry combat vehicles and (*right*) a 155mm GCT self-propelled gun. Variants of the AMX-10P were used by both the French and the Saudi armies, and the latter bought about 580 of them. It can carry up to eight infantrymen.

The Saudis also used the Brazilian Avibras Astros-II SS-30 multiple rocket system.

Saudi National Guardsmen examining a US M252 81mm mortar.

US combat engineers from the US 24th Infantry Division testing a mine plough attached to an M728 combat engineer vehicle. The latter was based on the M60 tank and was armed with a short-barrelled 165mm M135 demolition gun; normally fitted with a bulldozer blade, its role was to clear obstacles and prepare firing positions.

(*Above*) Saddam's attack on the Saudi town of Khafji was eventually thwarted by the Iraqi Army's lack of air cover. This hapless Iraqi tank was caught in the open. No Iraqi tanks succeeded in getting into Khafji, and the Iraqi armoured personnel carriers that did reach the town were quickly knocked out.

(*Opposite, top*) The remains of more knocked-out Iraqi tanks caught in the open.

(*Opposite, bottom*) A Royal Saudi Land Forces' Blackhawk photographed in the desert with two French helicopters.

A French VAB 4x4 armoured personnel carrier with HOT anti-tank missiles.

Five French AMX-10RC armoured cars putting on an impressive show of strength. This heavily armed yet fast reconnaissance vehicle was ideally suited to the open desert landscape.

Chapter Five

Saudi Counter-attack

If the Coalition had given Saddam any breathing space, there is every reason to believe that he could have turned Khafji into a stronghold defended by minefields and interlocking strongpoints incorporating the town's buildings. The coalition leaders knew from the Iran–Iraq War that the Iraqi Armed Forces were moderately competent on the offensive; of greater concern was the fact that they had conducted eight years of almost continuous defensive action against the Iranians. The Iraqi Army was skilled in constructing defensive positions and berms, establishing minefields and laying down artillery fire. Furthermore the Iraqi Navy might attempt to replenish the town under the cover of darkness.

The battle of Khafji was a matter of national prestige, and as this was Saudi soil it was felt that the Saudis, with support from Qatari troops, should be given the role of driving the Iraqis out. These forces were under the command of General Khalid, backed by US Marines and coalition air power. 'Two British advisers from the British Military Mission to the National Guard accompanied the engagement,' Ambassador Munro later admitted.

The counter-attack force included three mechanized SANG battalions and elements of a Saudi armoured battalion with supporting American tanks, backed by a Qatari armoured battalion equipped with about twenty tanks. The latter were paired up with seven tanks to each company of the 7th Battalion, 2nd SANG Brigade. The Qataris were to be kept in reserve: their lack of inter-communication with the Saudis, due to radio incompatibility, meant it was difficult to coordinate their efforts. The decision to deploy the National Guard may have been influenced not only by the fact that it was the most politically powerful arm of the Saudi military but because of its strong tribal roots and because it was considered more efficient than most Saudi Army formations; in addition, the situation in Khafji was arguably an internal security problem. However, the SANG, lacking tanks, could not have acted on its own.

Any force trundling across the flat open ground would be instantly spotted by Iraqi lookouts on the perimeter of the town. Indeed, during their approach the Saudis and Qataris found themselves under quite intense artillery shelling. American counter-battery fire detected and silenced the Iraqi guns. Ironically, two American Marines reconnaissance teams, some twelve men, still trapped in the town, acted as artillery observers for the besieging troops. They had at least one close call when an Iraqi patrol took shelter in a neighbouring room for several hours. Fortunately for the Coalition, the Marines were not discovered and continued to direct friendly fire into the environs and heart of Khafji.

Saudi progress was slow and hesitant, though they blamed the lack of adequate air support by the US Marines. Once the Cobra, Harrier and A-10 strikes got going they accounted for about thirty-five enemy tanks, alleviating the threat to the relief force. These air attacks also served to slow down the Saudis, who withdrew 2–3 kilometres every time there was an air engagement. On their initial advance the Saudis successfully secured the surrender of five Iraqi tanks and six APCs outside the town, their crews demoralized by the air strikes. Other units were not so keen to give up and one Saudi armoured vehicle was credited with knocking out eight Iraqi tanks.

In light of the Iraqi artillery fire, it was decided to launch the first assault under the cover of darkness, potentially a tricky operation despite the use of modern technology such as thermal imaging. On the night of 30/31 January the Saudi and Qatari forces (though they were largely Pakistanis serving in these units) moved up to their jump-off points. Coalition aircraft had silenced most of the Iraqi armour foolish enough to be visible beforehand. They also bombed two divisions of Saddam's 3rd Corps detected inside Kuwait gathering for a follow-on attack at Khafji. One strike by three American B-52 bombers reportedly destroyed eighty vehicles.

The 2nd SANG Brigade, supported by a company of the 8th RSLF Brigade, finally attacked Khafji itself at dusk, and Iraqi snipers promptly immobilized about ten of their wheeled armoured vehicles. In response the 8th RSLF's armour was brought up, pushing the Iraqis back. Under cover of a supporting barrage, the Saudis gained a lodgement in the southern end of the town. Inaccurate and sporadic small arms and anti-tank fire greeted the attack. Recovering quickly from the first clash, the Iraqis proved to be resilient and some of their remaining soldiers had to be cleared from the town's outlying buildings one by one. Nevertheless, in the chaos others quickly threw down their arms, perhaps realizing they were cut off and that resistance was now futile.

Just outside Khafji, Prince Khalid was concerned that the Iraqis might counter-attack and cut him off. He called up the air operations room in Riyadh and spoke to his own air force commander before being passed on to General Chuck Horner of the United States Air Force.

'I am worried,' confessed Khalid.

'We'll keep them off you,' Horner promised. He then added with a laugh, 'Khalid, I want you to keep one thing in mind.'

'What's that?' responded the prince.

'You're in a bunker in Khafji, and I'm here in Riyadh. It's easy for me to be calm!'

The Saudis' main two-pronged attack was launched the following day, with the 8th Mechanized Infantry Battalion/2nd SANG reinforced by the Qatari tanks and an anti-tank platoon on the right, and the 7th Battalion/2nd SANG on the left. Saudi Marines also moved up the coast road to secure the south. In the confusion the Qataris opened fire on SANG troops, though luckily there were no casualties.

On the second day of the battle the Saudis discovered that their M60 tanks outgunned the Iraqis' T-55s by 900 metres and their TOW missiles by 2,000 metres. The 7th Battalion advanced on the south of Khafji supported by the 3rd Marines and the Qataris. In the first clash inside Khafji itself the SANG suffered just one killed and four wounded. The Iraqis also managed to knock out three Saudi armoured vehicles with RPG-7 anti-tank weapons.

The 7th and 8th Battalions forced their way further into the town, fighting street by street for the rest of the morning. Iraqi forward observers operated from Khafji's water tower and as a result took a lot of incoming fire. Five Iraqi dead were found in and around it. During the fighting the Iraqis had called repeatedly for air support but the Iraqi Air Force stayed away. Coalition forces lost 19 dead and 36 wounded.

Meanwhile Saddam's follow-on forces at Wafra, as well as a 10-mile-long column passing through Kuwait, were attacked by coalition aircraft. They took heavy losses and were forced to retire. The US 1st Armored Division also used the Advanced Tactical Missile System on Iraqi targets. At Wafra the Iraqis lost 33 tanks and 38 APCs, whilst the Americans took 11 Iraqi POWs and suffered 11 dead and 2 wounded. Saddam Hussein was unable to bring up his Republican Guard units as reinforcements as they were under aerial siege. In a twenty-four hour period they endured 350 tactical strikes and 10 B-52 attacks. On 1 February they were on the receiving end of another 600 sorties. Saddam's fist in Khafji was on its own.

To the north of Khafji an Iraqi brigade with a hundred armoured vehicles tried pushing south but twelve of its vehicles were destroyed when they were engaged by the Saudi TOW platoon from the 8th RSLF Brigade for half an hour. The Iraqis were then harried back by coalition aircraft; both those forces trying to reinforce Khafji and those attacking to the west suffered from air attack. Iraqis fleeing north from Khafji lost another dozen tanks. The US Marines countered an Iraqi armoured battalion making a diversionary attack 80km to the west near Umm Hujul.

On the third day the fighting for Khafji lasted twelve hours. When eventually the Iraqi snipers had been silenced, it was discovered that in and around the town the Iraqis had lost at least 40 dead (some reports state as many as 300, and it is thought the Saudis may have played down the death toll), 35 wounded, 463 prisoners and up to 80 armoured vehicles. Several of Saddam's Chinese-built YW-531 APCs were found knocked out in the streets, lost either to the Coalition's fighter-bombers or to artillery fire.

'The fighting was vividly recorded on Saudi television,' recalled Ambassador Munro, and 'General Khalid was able on 1 February to claim a significant victory for Saudi forces.' The Saudi press agency issued a triumphant statement saying Khafji had been 'cleansed completely of aggressive forces'.

The entire Iraqi garrison had been destroyed. In three days the Saudi forces lost eighteen men killed and thirty-two wounded, as well as three tanks and a TOW launcher. During the same period, according to the Saudis, the Iraqis lost eleven tanks and fifty-one APCs destroyed, and nineteen APCs captured. In addition, the Saudis bagged a total of 1,040 PoWs. It was interesting that the Iraqi heavy equipment captured at Khafji showed evidence of poor maintenance. General Schwarzkopf later recalled, 'From Iraq's standpoint, the battle for Khafji was a debacle. The 5th Mechanized Division, which had been rated one of their finest armoured units, just a notch below the Republican Guard, was almost entirely destroyed – we monitored Iraqi reports afterwards that indicated that only 20 per cent of that division made it back. During the battle Iraq's highly vaunted artillery had proved ineffective – they had fired hundreds of rounds but never succeeded in zeroing in on our troops.'

First blood had gone to the coalition forces and the SANG had given a good if patchy account of itself. Furthermore, the Coalition was able to heave a sigh of relief that the urban battlefield had not turned into a costly bloodbath and a media disaster. This proved a major morale boost for the untried Saudi armed forces and showed they could conduct themselves well.

A Saudi spokesman, Colonel Ahmed Al-Robayan, stated that the success of the combined arms operation against the Iraqis at Khafji was a 'very good sign' as it tested the command and control systems of the multi-national force. 'The Saudi forces are doing an outstanding job,' commented Marine Brigadier General Richard Neal, Deputy Director of US Central Command operations, adding 'They did a terrific job at Khafji . . . I've been impressed with them.'

Although it was perhaps only a minor engagement in the overall scheme of things, Khafji echoed German attempts to move their armour to the Normandy bridgehead in 1944. If Saddam could have widened the battle by bringing up his follow-on forces and offered some token air cover, the fight may not have gone so well for the Coalition. It is possible that the Americans would have had to divert more troops to help the SAAF, distracting them from the left hook. Without air support, the Iraqis' offensive manoeuvring was totally compromised and thus they fought a largely defensive battle. Air power and artillery dominated at Khafji, and remained dominant aspects of the whole campaign.

However, the battle at Khafji proved that Saddam Hussein could achieve limited tactical surprise, and his forces' stout resistance once in the town was a propaganda victory for him. It took the Saudis three days to fully secure Khafji and they quickly discovered their wheeled armoured vehicles were inadequate for the job. Nonetheless, Saddam's first strike failed with heavy losses and demonstrated that his forces were extremely vulnerable to air attack. His gamble did not pay off. If Saddam had picked a better place, concentrated his forces more quickly and attacked more effectively, he might have seriously disrupted the Coalition's plans. While Saddam claimed the battle at Khafji as a great victory, Coalition commander General Schwarzkopf recalled it as the occasion when he 'really began to think we were going to kick this guy's tail'.

Royal Saudi Land Forces' armoured personnel carriers and tanks moving up through a cleared minefield ready for the big offensive. At Khafji the job fell to the well-equipped Saudi National Guard.

A V-150 Commando APC of the Saudi Arabian National Guard during the battle for Khafji. This turretless version mounts a .50 calibre M2 machine gun. Several of these APCs were lost during the battle at the end of January 1991.

A Saudi Arabian Tornado prepares to take off on a mission during Desert Storm.

Flight-deck crewmen aboard the amphibious assault ship USS *Nassau* (LHA-4) refuel two Marine Corps' McDonnell/BAe AV-8B Harrier II aircraft as a third Harrier comes in to land. The Harriers provided vital close-air support for the Marines onshore.

A Grumman A-6E Intruder attack aircraft flies over the desert as it prepares for refuelling. The Iraqis managed to hit several such aircraft with ground fire, resulting in at least one having to be scrapped.

Lacking air support, this was the fate of much of Saddam's armour at Khafji. Visible are the blackened remains of Soviet-built BMP infantry fighting vehicles and a T-54 tank. The Coalition had almost complete air supremacy, meaning the Iraqi Army had little freedom of manoeuvre. All Iraqi troop concentrations were swiftly and ruthlessly bombed.

Saudi military personnel being transported in an M113 armoured personnel carrier armed with an M-2 .50-calibre general purpose heavy machine gun.

A Royal Saudi Air Force F-15 Eagle fighter aircraft approaches a KC-135 Stratotanker from the 1700th Air Refuelling Squadron Provisional for air-to-air refuelling. The standard short-range weapon carried by this aircraft was the AIM-9M Sidewinder missile. The Saudis had F-15 squadrons based at Dhahran and Taif.

Chapter Six

Obliterating Saddam's Navy

After 2 August 1990, once Iraq had overrun its hapless former ally, Iraqi naval patrol boats were able to slip out of Umm Qasr and down the coast between Kuwait and Bubiyan Island. Iraq quickly secured the naval bases at Al Ahmadi, south of Kuwait City, and Shuwaikh, capturing most of the Kuwaiti Navy intact. Kuwait had some twenty-three patrol boats and coastal vessels, the most significant of which were six German-built TNC-45s and two German FPB-57 missile patrol boats equipped with MM-40 Exocet missiles. Some of these were pressed into service to support the Iraqi attack on Khafji almost six months later, but the Iraqi Navy was little more than a bit player during Desert Storm.

RAF Jaguar jets roaring over the Bubiyan Channel in early 1991 caught Saddam's navy bloodied and fleeing the fight; with nowhere to hide the outcome was predictable. The Kuwaiti island of Bubiyan was the very *raison d'être* of the Iraqi fleet, but once in Saddam's possession it heralded the Iraqi Navy's death knell. Saddam's naval forces had always been the poor cousin to his powerful army and air force. Geography had seen to this: Iraq is largely a landlocked nation, although it has a small outlet into the Gulf and part of its eastern border with Iran runs along the infamous Shatt-al-Arab Waterway.

By the time the preliminary air campaign for Desert Storm opened in mid-January 1991, the Coalition had already started clearing the Iraqi maritime presence in the adjacent area of the Gulf around Kuwait. Although the bulk of the air effort was directed at the Iraqi Army, the Republican Guard and the Iraqi Air Force, Saddam's navy must have been surprised by the intensity and tempo of the attacks it endured. The Coalition assessed Iraq's most dangerous naval assets to be the Exocet-armed ex-Kuwaiti TNC-45s and the Russian-built Osas armed with Styx missiles (deemed an effective threat against surface targets), and their lower-capability Zhuks or patrol boats. It was decided to hunt these down as quickly as possible.

Coalition air attacks hit and disabled Iraq's training frigate, and regular raids were launched against Umm Qasr on 21 January. One of the Iraqi Navy's roles was to evacuate its troops off the nearby islands and oil platforms once they discovered how vulnerable they were to air attack. During one of these operations a suspected

Iraqi minelayer was disabled near the Kuwaiti island of Qaruh, which was recaptured on 24 January. Despite these air attacks, the Iraqi Navy was instructed to assist with a probing attack on Saudi Arabia.

Iraq's naval aspirations were constrained by the size of its coastline beyond the Shatt-al-Arab Waterway. Running to the west, Iraq has just 25km of coast; in contrast, tiny neighbouring Kuwait has 180km of coastline, plus the strategic islands of Warbah and Bubiyan, which dominate the estuary leading to the Iraqi port of Umm Qasr, and a large natural harbour north of Kuwait City. This situation was a source of constant friction.

In the late 1950s and early 1960s Moscow provided Baghdad with 12 P-6 torpedo boats, 6 smaller patrol boats and 3 SO-1 submarine chasers. Britain also supplied Iraq with six patrol boats. Iraq's naval acquisitions paled into insignificance, though, compared to the vast array of larger warships that Iran was obtaining at the time, which included a destroyer and a number of corvettes. What the Iraqis needed was a force multiplier, and they found it in the shape of Soviet missile patrol boats, which were considered revolutionary when they appeared in the early 1950s. Torpedo boats were becoming increasingly vulnerable, as the North Vietnamese Navy (NVN) discovered in the early 1960s. Interestingly, while Moscow chose not to arm the NVN with missile boats, it looked upon Baghdad more favourably.

Initial Iraqi naval imports were followed by four Soviet Osa-I and three Osa-II missile patrol craft, each armed with four SSN-2 Styx ship-to-ship missile (SSM) launchers. This created an effective fledgling Iraqi Navy based at Basra on the Shatt-al-Arab Waterway and at Umm Qasr, just north of the Kuwaiti border. This development was a concern to both the Kuwaitis and Iranians as the Styx, with its 12-mile range, could be used to attack coastal targets, despite being primarily an anti-shipping weapon.

During 1975 and 1976 Iraq received five additional Soviet Osa-IIs, and the Iraqis were so enamoured of the Styx missile that they began to develop their own indigenous versions. As far as Saddam was concerned, missile patrol boats were just the start of things. He had vastly more ambitious aspirations for his fledgling fleet: he wanted major surface combatants. His programme of major warship acquisition became apparent in 1979, when a contract was signed with Yugoslavia to supply a 1,850-ton training frigate, which was duly delivered in the early 1980s. Throughout the late 1970s Saddam courted the major warship manufacturers, for he planned to acquire a navy that could take on Iran's.

Saddam revealed the scale of his accelerated expansion programme for the Iraqi Navy in early 1980, when he ordered no fewer than 11 ships: 4 Lupo class frigates (dubbed *Hittin* by the Iraqis), 6 Wadi class corvettes (*Assad* or *Hussa el Hussair*), and a Stromboli class (*Agnadeen*) support ship from Italy worth $1.5 billion. To equip these vessels, Iraq also ordered two A-109 and five AB-212 anti-submarine warfare helicopters, as well as Albatross, Aspide and Otomat-2 ship-to-ship missiles. Iraqi oil dollars ensured that Saddam could obtain the best that money could buy.

When the Iran–Iraq War broke out, the Iraqi Navy numbered just 4,250 men, of whom 3,200 were conscripts. They could pit just 5 ex-Soviet large patrol craft (3 SO-1s and 2 Poluchats), 12 Osa fast attack craft (4 Osa-Is and 8 Osa-IIs) and 12 P-6 fast attack craft armed with torpedoes against the Iranian fleet. The latter, built up by the Shah, was 20,000-strong and equipped with 3 destroyers, 4 frigates, 4 corvettes, 9 FAC(M)s and 14 hovercraft. During the war the Iraqi Navy spent most of its time holed up in its bases. It played a very limited role in the 'Tanker War', conducted in the Gulf with gusto by the air forces of both sides, though Iraqi patrol boats were used to fend off Iranian naval commando attacks on Iraqi oil platforms. In the mid-1980s China supplied Saddam with possibly more than a hundred Hai Ying-1/2 (HY-1/2) coastal defence missiles to arm Iraq's Osa-IIs and its B-6 bombers (the Chinese version of the Soviet Tu-16). Essentially copies of the Soviet Styx, the HY-1/2 missiles were designated by the West the CSSC-3 Silkworm and Seersucker respectively. Some thirty Chinese C-601 anti-ship missiles were also provided. Egypt, a staunch Iraqi ally, may have provided additional HY-2s as well.

By the time the war came to an end, on paper the Iraqi Navy had 5 frigates and 38 patrol and coastal combatants, including 4 corvettes. However, the four *Hittin* frigates, four *Hussa el Hussair* corvettes and the *Agnadeen* support ship remained stranded in Italy. The remaining frigate, *Khaldoum*, was a training vessel, so in effect the Iraqi Navy's assault arm really only consisted of eight Osas and six P-6 FACs, supported by eight mine warfare vessels and six amphibious support boats (comprising three *Al Zahraa*s and three ex-Soviet Polnocny landing ships).

After the cease-fire with Iran, Saddam moved quickly to clear the ports of Umm Qasr and Khor al-Zubair, demanding that the seventy-five commercial ships trapped in the Shatt-al-Arab Waterway be moved. In 1989 Saddam sought to give Iraq a stronger anti-shipping arm by ordering six French AS-332 Super Puma helicopters armed with thirty-six AM-39 Exocet missiles and six AS-365N Dauphine helicopters armed with forty-eight AS-15TT missiles (along with 350 AS-30L anti-ship missiles for its Mirage F-1s). Luckily for the Coalition, they were not delivered in time for the Gulf War. Nonetheless by this stage Iraq was itself producing versions of the Styx known as the Faw-70/150 and 200. Iraq also came up with another way to expand its naval capabilities.

On the night of 29 January 1991 elements of the Iraqi Army's 5th Mechanized Division moved out over a 50-mile front to attack the Saudi town of Khafji. They crossed the Kuwaiti border undetected and pushed south, supported by seventeen fast patrol boats, which moved down the coast bearing landing parties. RAF Jaguars, operating out of Muharraq in Bahrain, pounced on the naval element of the assault, hitting at least two of the vessels, including a landing craft which is believed to have sunk, and scattering the rest. The Royal Navy also got in on the act and on the same day attacked some Iraqi patrol boats that may have been heading for the Khafji operation or were simply trying to flee to Iran. British warships detected the boats and launched Lynx helicopters armed with Sea Skua missiles. In total, twenty-five missiles were fired, of which eighteen hit their targets. Seven vessels were sunk and hits were registered on a number of other smaller boats.

Rather foolishly, the following day a second convoy appeared; it included an Iraqi T-43 class minesweeper, 3 ex-Kuwaiti TNC-45 fast attack boats and 3 Polnocny landing ships. RAF Jaguar and USAF A-6 jets set about them. In the desperate Battle of Bubiyan Island twenty Iraqi naval craft attempted to run the channel between Bubiyan and Warbah into Iranian waters. Chase was given and a turkey shoot followed; only two damaged vessels – a patrol boat and an amphibious ship – managed to escape the deluge of bombs and missiles laid down on them. By 2 February 1991 the Iraqi Navy was assessed to be incapable of mounting any further offensive action.

With Kuwaiti waters secured, US battleships began to fire on Iraqi shore defences around Kuwait City on 23 February and the following day the ground war commenced. Iraqi naval defences were not quite finished, however, for on 25 February two Silkworm missiles were fired at coalition ships. One was shot down by HMS *Gloucester*'s Sea Dart system and the other crashed ignominiously into the Gulf. During the whole war twenty Iraqi naval targets suffered 247 air strikes. The only damage to coalition naval forces was due to mines. The Iraqi Navy was no more.

The first salvo of sea-launched Tomahawk Land Attack Missiles (TLAMs) was fired by the cruiser USS *San Jacinto* on 17 January 1991, followed by the attack submarines USS *Pittsburgh* and USS *Louisville*. In total, 288 TLAMs were launched against Iraqi targets.

The Ticonderoga-class cruiser USS *San Jacinto* was commissioned in 1988 and deployed to the Gulf with a full load of 122 Tomahawk missiles in 1991. The vessel fired a total of sixteen missiles.

Laser-guided bombs on the flight-deck of the carrier USS *John F. Kennedy* in preparation for air strikes against Irac. The A-6E Intruder in the background is also armed with laser-guided bombs.

A boarding party from the guided missile destroyer USS *Goldsborough* (DDG-20) board an Iraqi general dry cargo ship to search for contraband during Operation Desert Shield.

A Tornado Air Defence Variant launching a Sky Flash air-to-air missile. On the whole the Iraqi Air Force simply melted away in the face of such air power.

While the Iraqi Navy posed no real threat to the Coalition, Iraqi mines were another matter. The amphibious assault ship USS *Tripoli* (LPH-10) struck a mine while on mine-clearing duties in the northern Persian Gulf on 18 February 1991. The blast holed the vessel below the waterline.

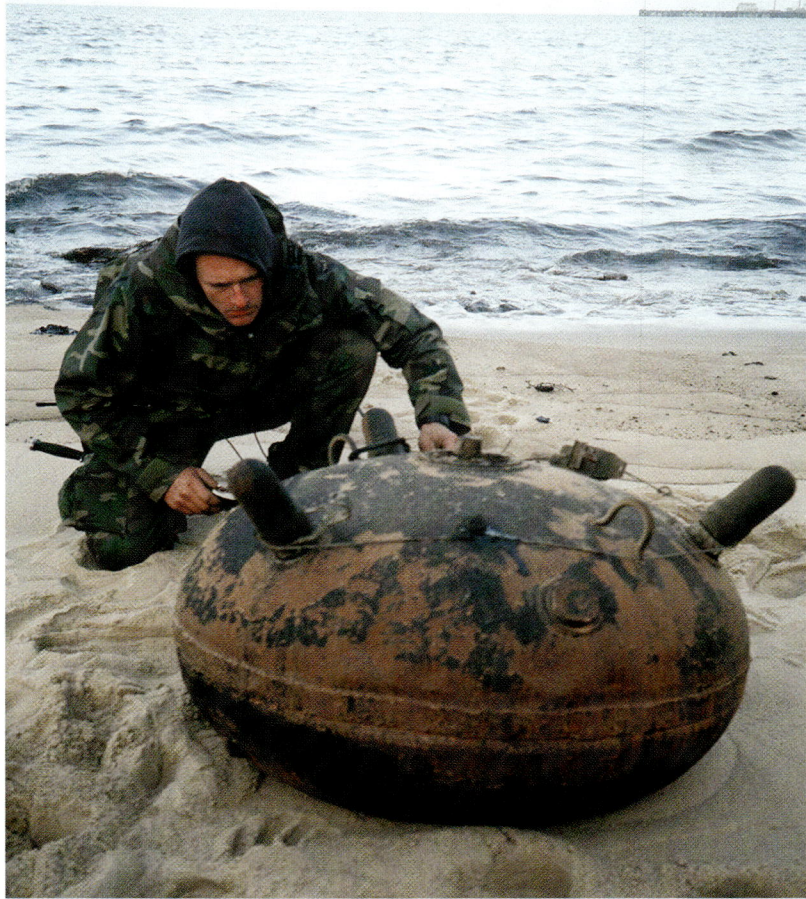

A US EOD specialist examines a washed-up Iraqi contact mine.

A Tornado F33 aircraft of the Royal Saudi Air Force taking off during Operation Desert Shield.

F-14A Tomcats from Fighter Squadron 14 (VF-14) and Fighter Squadron 33 (VF-33) rendezvous with a KC-10A Extender aircraft for in-flight refuelling while on patrol in the Gulf. VF-14 operated from the aircraft carrier USS *John F. Kennedy* (CV-67), while VF-33 flew from the carrier USS *America* (CV-66).

USS *America* returning to Norfolk, Virginia, following her deployment in the Persian Gulf during Operation Desert Storm.

Chapter Seven

Desert Sabre

General Schwarzkopf knew that speed was of the essence in the ground war. He had to conduct two envelopments, the first around Kuwait to prevent the Iraqi garrison escaping, and a second much larger one to prevent reinforcements reaching Kuwait. He also needed to secure Kuwait's vital oilfields as quickly as possible – there were three major areas in the north-east and four to the south. Saddam's generals planned to use oil as an environmental weapon that would enhance their defences and funnel their enemy's tanks into predetermined killing zones. Once Schwarzkopf's attack started, there was every chance that Saddam's generals would open up the valves in Kuwait's oilfields to form vast oil lakes and dynamite the oilheads to create seas of fire and choking smoke. This would greatly impede the Coalition's tanks and jets; it would also hide any Iraqi troops massing for a counter-attack. Oil industry experts anticipated that up to 150 oil wells would be destroyed during the fighting.

Schwarzkopf and his commanders had every reason to be concerned about the fate of Kuwait's oilfields. Saddam's generals had in place a massive scorched earth plan that would set fire to over 600 oil wells in the face of Schwarzkopf's offensive. This would result in the loss of six million barrels of oil a day and billowing smoke rising to over 10,000ft. The oil that was not burned off would create 300 oil lakes holding up to 50 million barrels of oil. The sand, gravel, oil and soot would result in almost 5 per cent of Kuwait covered in a layer of 'tarcrete', which would clog up the tracks of Schwarzkopf's tanks. For good measure the Iraqis also sowed minefields around the oilfields so that firefighters would not be able to reach the blazing wells. This represented an appalling environmental disaster and would create a hellish battlefielc straight from Dante's *Inferno*.

Schwarzkopf fully understood that his tanks had to dash forward as fast as possible to try to prevent this, but ultimately it would prove to be an impossible task. Even before the ground war commenced in late January, Saddam's men had sabotaged Kuwait's main supertanker loading pier, dumping 460 million gallons of crude oil into the Gulf. They also set fire to the oil wells and storage tanks at Wafra. By mid-February about fifty oil wells were damaged or on fire due to coalition air attacks on Iraqi forces stationed in the oilfields. Then on 16 February, perhaps anticipating the attack, the Iraqis began systematically wrecking hundreds of Kuwaiti oilfields, as well as sinking five oil tankers anchored off the Kuwait coast. It was clear that once the Iraqi Army was being driven from Kuwait, the destruction would only get worse.

Therefore Schwarzkopf's ground offensive, dubbed Operation Desert Sabre, envisaged an enormous encircling operation that would encompass not only Kuwait but also a vast area of southern Iraq stretching up almost to the city of Basra. Although King Fahd was commander-in-chief SAAF, operational control of all Arab forces came under his nephew, His Royal Highness Lieutenant General Prince Khalid bin Sultan (the son of Prince Sultan bin Abdul Aziz, the Saudi Defence Minister). Egyptian and Syrian forces were also committed to the offensive, on the proviso they were not used inside Iraq.

Three commands were deployed on the eastern third of this enormous front. These consisted of the Joint Forces Command North, made up of the units from Egypt, Syria and Saudi Arabia, led by Lieutenant General Prince Khalid bin Sultan, which held the portion of the line east of VII Corps. To the right of these forces was Lieutenant General Walter E. Boomer's US 1st Marine Expeditionary Force, which included the 1st (Tiger) Brigade of the Army's US 2nd Armored Division, as well as the US 1st and 2nd Marine Divisions. On the extreme right Joint Forces Command East, anchoring the line on the Gulf, consisted of units from all six member states of the Gulf Co-operation Council. Like Joint Forces Command North, it was under General Khalid's command.

The two US Marine divisions, with the US Army's Tiger Brigade, and coalition forces under Saudi command were to push directly north into Kuwait. These forces would hold the enemy's tactical and operational forces in place by breaching the Iraqi defences in Kuwait and encircling the Iraqi forces in the heel of Kuwait and Kuwait City. Once Kuwait City was encircled and Iraqi forces were driven out or defeated, the Arab forces would then liberate Kuwait City itself.

To the west the XVIII Airborne Corps was to attack deep into Iraq to control the east–west lines of communication along the strategic Highway 8 and cut off Iraqi forces in the Kuwait Theatre of Operations. Even further west, the French 6th Light Armoured Division and the US 101st Airborne Division were to conduct a massive western envelopment, with a ground assault to secure the coalition's left flank and an air assault to establish forward support bases deep in Iraqi territory. The US 24th Infantry Division had the central role of blocking the Euphrates river valley to prevent the escape north of Iraqi forces in Kuwait, and then attacking east in coordination with VII Corps to defeat the armour-heavy divisions of the Republican Guard.

In the centre of the coalition line, along the Wadi al-Batin, Brigadier General John H. Tilelli's US 1st Cavalry Division was to strike north into a concentration of Iraqi divisions, whose commanders remained convinced that the Coalition would use Batin and several other wadis as avenues of attack. In the meantime VII Corps would conduct the main coalition effort, attacking east of XVIII Airborne Corps and west of Wadi al-Batin, driving first north and then east to find and destroy the heart of Saddam's ground forces, the armour-heavy Republican Guard divisions.

Desert Sabre was unleashed at 0400 hours on 24 February 1991. The Iraqi Army in the KTO knew that Saddam had abandoned them, and many soldiers had little desire to fght for him once the enemy armour came into their sights. The relentless air attacks had already taken a terrible toll on Iraqi morale. Washington assessed that at least 150,000 Iraqi troops had deserted before Desert Sabre even commenced. Two Iraqi divisional commanders subsequently informed their British captors that they had received no orders for almost two weeks.

As instructed, Joint Force Command East (comprising Saudi, Kuwaiti, Omani and UAE forces) pushed towards Kuwait up the coastal route to form the anvil for the American, British and French hammer-blow assault into Iraq, which was to trap the bulk of the Iraqi forces in the KTO. The Saudis came up against the Iraqi 5th Mechanized Division, still recovering from the Khafji encounter, while Commander Marine Central (MARCENT) breached Iraqi defences further inland.

To the far west, as planned, General Mouscardes's French 6th Light Armoured Division, reinforced by the 2nd Brigade of the US 82nd Airborne Division, advanced to protect the far western flank. The 82nd was bolstered with forty-three M551A1 Sheridan light airborne assault vehicles in its air-droppable tank battalion. The French 4th Dragoon Regiment, normally part of the French 10th Armoured Division, was augmented by elements of the 503rd Combat Tank Regiment. French reconnaissance units consisted of the 1st Foreign Legion Cavalry Regiment and the 1st Spahis Regiment; both were capable of conducting such offensive operations as they had strong anti-tank capabilities. They consisted of three squadrons equipped with AMX-10RC 6x6 armoured cars, armed with the 105mm gun, plus the Véhicule de l'Avant Blindé (VAB) 4x4 armoured personnel carrier. Both were ideal for the mad dash across the Iraqi desert. None of the newer tracked AMX-10P infantry combat vehicles was deployed to the Gulf. Mouscardes's men moved to successfully secure the Al-Salman air base. Pushing almost 65km into Iraq, they destroyed the Iraqi 45th Infantry Division, then formed a screen to protect the left flank of the XVIII Airborne Corps assault. Fortunately for the French they suffered few casualties, with only three fatalities in combat.

To their east some 2,000 men of General Peay's US 101st Airborne Division were moved forward in a massive air-lift involving 400 helicopters. Some 110km inside

Iraq they established a forward operating base named Cobra. A further 2,000 men arrived by vehicle, then the division moved to secure vital roads along the Euphrates and Tigris valleys to isolate the Iraqi forces in Kuwait. Meanwhile, XVIII Corps' US 24th Infantry Division under General McCaffrey, supported by the US 3rd Armoured Cavalry Regiment, raced north to link up with the 101st, and on 25 February swung right to attack the northernmost Iraqi Republican Guard positions. The 3rd Cavalry was the only tank unit equipped with the M1A1 Abrams, and was the first US unit to take on the Iraqis in an engagement on 22 January 1991.

Saddam Hussein, probably realizing that defeat in Kuwait was inevitable, sought to protect his regime, but this hampered his generals. Key units were held back and he was reluctant to risk either the Republican Guard or his air force. In senior circles the Iraqi Army probably understood that it was not to make a last stand in the deserts of Kuwait and southern Iraq, but rather retreat to try to save Saddam's regime. Saddam may have also underestimated the defensive abilities of the Iraqi Army as a result of the Iran–Iraq War. The Iranian Army had been ill-equipped and poorly trained and led, resulting in appalling casualties for little ground gained. Saddam initially hoped that his forces would inflict unacceptable casualties on the Coalition and score a propaganda coup as well as an early cessation of hostilities.

In the meantime US armoured columns raced to trap the Republican Guard and prevent them escaping northwest towards Baghdad with their armour. Initially the Iraqi commanders thought VII Corps was driving on Kuwait City, not against the Guard itself. The intention had been that the Iraqi 12th Armoured Division would act as the immediate tactical reserve, while the Guard forming the strategic reserve came to the rescue. When the Guard realized what was happening, they desperately attempted to stop VII Corps from breaking through to their rear. Three elite divisions, the Medina, Hammurabi and Tawakalna, deployed by the road running parallel to the Iraqi–Saudi pipeline.

The scene was set for the battle for Kuwait City and the battle of the Basra pocket.

General Schwarzkopf, commander-in-chief US Central Command, briefs his troops during Operation Desert Shield. For him speed was of the essence in the ground war, to keep the Iraqi armed forces off balance.

Lieutenant General Khalid Bin Sultan Bin Abdul Aziz commanded all the Arab forces within the Coalition and worked closely with General Schwarzkopf.

In a scene reminiscent of the Second World War or the Arab–Israeli Wars, an American co umn protected by Abrams tanks and Bradley infantry fighting vehicles (IFVs) prepares for the offensive.

An Abrams kicks up the dust. This tank won its spurs during Operation Desert Sabre. Of the 1,955 M1A1 Abrams tanks in theatre, 4 were disabled and 4 were damaged but repairable. No M1A1 crew members were killed by enemy fire in the many tank engagements.

A US Brady IFV poised for battle. Of the 2,200 Bradleys in theatre, only 3 were disabled.

Blazing Iraqi Type 59 or 69 tanks. Those that were not caught by coalition air strikes were picked off at long range by coalition armour. These ones suffered at the hands of the British 1st Armoured Division's gunnery.

An Iraqi T-62 main battle tank destroyed near the Ali Al Salem air base during Operation Desert Storm.

Nigerien soldiers. Niger sent a 400-man military contingent to support the American-led Coalition against Iraq.

A pair of AMX-30 main battle tanks and a truck belonging to the French 6th Light Armoured Division pause outside Al-Salman. The tanks have a sand and olive-green camouflage scheme that does not extend to the road wheels.

Soldiers examine an Iraqi T-55 tank destroyed by the French 6th Light Armoured Division. This tank also seems to have a camouflage scheme.

On the right men of the US 1st Cavalry Division work on an AH-64A Apache helicopter, while to the left soldiers examine a captured Iraqi Mi-25 Hind-D helicopter.

A destroyed Iraqi T-55 tank stands in the sand at Jalibah airfield. Despite being hulled down, the scorching on the left indicates the tank was hit side on.

Armoured Amphibious Assault Vehicles (LVTP-7s) belonging to the US Marine Corps. They launched a diversionary attack towards Kuwait City that succeeded in liberating the airport despite fierce resistance.

This M60A1, serving with the US Marines Company D, 2nd Tank Battalion, formed part of Task Force Breach Alpha. The tank is fitted with reactive armour and an M-9 bulldozer kit.

More wrecked Iraqi tanks.

US Marine gunners preparing their M-198 155mm howitzer for a fire mission against Iraqi positions during Operation Desert Sabre.

The Niger Army's French-built Panhard AML light armoured cars, armed with 90mm guns, in a holding area during Operation Desert Shield.

Chapter Eight

Desert Rats

In mid-January 1991 it was assessed that facing General de la Billiere's British 1st Armoured Division were seven Iraqi divisions, consisting of the 20th, 21st and 25th Infantry Divisions, with the 6th, 12th and 17th Armoured Divisions and the Tawakalna Republican Guard Division in reserve. By the end of January the Iraqi 16th Infantry Division had joined the front-line forces and the reserves were bolstered by the 26th and 36th Infantry Divisions. On paper this was a formidably daunting force. However, the front-line divisions had no overhead cover and were suffering daily under the air strikes. Nonetheless Britain's armoured forces were about to become involved in some fierce tank battles.

Just before the start of the ground offensive, coalition Special Forces were sent on Scud missile hunting missions. Aside from the extreme dangers posed by Saddam's chemical weapons, another particular threat faced by the Coalition's ground troops was his considerable arsenal of tactical ballistic missiles. These had successfully rained down death and destruction on Iran's cities during the Iran–Iraq War.

British special operations were the responsibility of the 22nd Special Air Service (SAS) Regiment and their naval counterparts in the Special Boat Service (SBS). The SAS deployed out of their depot at Hereford, Cyprus and Oman. However, a few SAS members were already in Kuwait, having been assigned to the British Military Assistance Training team advising the Kuwaiti Army at the time of Saddam's invasion. These men were able to provide invaluable intelligence on the local conditions. Using their well-honed covert tactics, SAS patrols roamed the rear areas in their Landrover Desert Patrol Vehicles ('Pink Panthers') and their Longline Light Strike Vehicles. On 7 January 1991 US and British Special Forces raided an Iraqi air defence missile site and made off with a Soviet-manufactured radar system. The SBS cooperated with their American cousins, the US Navy SEALs, who were given responsibility for the Kuwait City area.

Coalition commanders were very aware of the threat posed by Iraqi missiles. Saddam had first fired his Soviet-made Scud-B missiles at Iran in 1982; this culminated six years later in the 'War of the Cities', in which both sides lobbed hundreds of missiles at each other. The enormity of this should not be underestimated: Saddam's bombardment in 1988 caused 8,000 Iranian casualties and drove out a quarter of Tehran's population. A decade later Iran targeted with missiles Iranian opposition forces that were being sheltered by Saddam.

By the time of the invasion of Kuwait, Saddam still had stocks of Scud-B missiles plus Iraqi modified variants known as the Al-Abbas, Al-Hussein and Al-Hijarah. In the build-up to the war forty-six Iraqi Scuds were fired at Saudi Arabia and another forty-two at Israel. One particular strike against a barracks at Dhahran in Saudi killed twenty-eight members of a US Army unit.

In support of Desert Sabre, Special Forces were tasked with gathering intelligence about the missiles, to vector in air strikes or if necessary destroy Saddam's missile launchers themselves. The most famous of these was the British SAS mission codenamed Bravo Two Zero. Despite Operation Desert Storm, few of Saddam's Scud launchers had been destroyed by coalition aircraft; Special Forces and coalition pilots claimed up to hundred launchers destroyed, but this figure was never substantiated.

Meanwhile, as part of Operation Granby, the British 1st Armoured Division, commanded by Major General Rupert Smith, came under the US VII Corps and was part of the great armoured left-hook that attacked the Iraqi Republican Guard formations. Smith's two brigades (the 4th and 7th, under Brigadiers Christopher Hammerbeck and Patrick Cordingley respectively) were to alternate spearheading the advance. In the vanguard of General Smith's assault were two armoured reconnaissance units. The British Army had continued its love affair with its cavalry regiments and remained wedded to the concept of reconnaissance by force. Dashing forward across the barren desert landscape, they were to probe the Iraqi defences that had withstood air attack and the preliminary artillery and rocket bombardment. Their highly dangerous job was to draw enemy fire to help locate positions that needed to be neutralized as the division rolled forwards. The firepower of these reconnaissance forces was quite considerable.

The chosen units were the 7th Armoured Brigade's A Squadron, 1st Queen's Dragoon Guards, and the divisional formation 16th/5th Queen's Royal Lancers Regiment. Whilst most countries opted for wheeled vehicles to conduct this role, the British Army had developed a unique family of tracked armoured fighting vehicles known as combat vehicle reconnaissance tracked (CVR(T)s). The two main variants were the FV101 Scorpion and FV107 Scimitar light tanks armed with 76mm and 30mm guns respectively. The headquarter elements were equipped with the anti-tank Striker variant and the Spartan armoured personnel carrier, both based on the Scorpion chassis. Also in support were Sultan command vehicles, Samson recovery vehicles and Samson ambulances, again all of which are Scorpion derivatives.

The light armour was to precede the heavy tank regiments, which consisted of the 7th Armoured Brigade's Royal Scots Dragoon Guards, reinforced by elements of the 14th/20th King's Hussars, 17th/21st Lancers and the 4th Royal Tank Regiment, and the Queen's Royal Irish Hussars tank regiment, also reinforced by units from the 17th/21st Lancers. The 4th Armoured Brigade's tank force comprised the 14th/20th Hussars Tank Regiment, reinforced by the Life Guards' A Squadron and elements of the 4th Tank Regiment. The Royal Scots Dragoon Guards and the Queen's Royal Irish Hussars had four tank squadrons totalling 57 Challenger tanks and 670 men, while the 14th/20th King's Hussars had three squadrons with 43 tanks and 650 men. The squadrons each had four tank troops, each with three tanks plus two in the HQ and administration troop.

In 1988 Brigadier Cordingley was given command of the 7th Armoured Brigade, comprising 5,000 men serving with the tank regiments, armoured infantry, artillery, engineers and support services. Two years later, in September 1990, with his force's strength now increased to 12,000 men, he took his brigade to Saudi Arabia as Britain's initial ground contribution to the Gulf War. The 7th Armoured Brigade had had an interesting history. In early 1940, when the British Mobile Division became the 7th Armoured Division, the Light Armoured Brigade was slightly confusingly redesignated the 7th Armoured Brigade. Nicknamed the 'Green Rats' or the 'Jungle Rats' after a deployment to Burma in 1942, the brigade then served in the Middle East before fighting in Italy for the rest of the Second World War. When the 7th Armoured Division (the 'Desert Rats') was disbanded in 1958, the 7th Armoured Brigade adopted its insignia and nickname. It formed part of the 1st (UK) Armoured Division when this was formed in 1976. After being briefly converted to Task Force Alpha in the late 1970s, the brigade was reinstated in 1981.

Each of the British armoured brigades had a field regiment with twenty-four 155mm M109A2 self-propelled howitzers, as well as an air defence missile battery with thirty-six Javelins, while divisional support came from the 26th Field Regiment with another twelve M109A2s. The 32nd Heavy Regiment was armed with sixteen M109A2s and twelve 203mm M110A1 self-propelled howitzers, and the 39th Heavy Regiment deployed twelve M270 Multiple Launch Rocket Systems. Tactical air support was supplied by the 4th Regiment, Army Air Corps, deployed with twenty-four Lynx AH Mk1 attack helicopters plus twenty-four French-designed but British-built Gazelle AH Mk1 scouts.

Late in the afternoon of 24 February 1991 VII Corps, comprising the main British and American forces, launched the central coalition thrust. The US 1st Infantry Division breached the defences. The battered and bruised Iraqi 48th Infantry Division in the mouth of the breach was estimated to have lost 98 per cent of its tanks – in other words it was wiped out as a fighting force. To the left of MARCENT, the Egyptian–Syrian Joint Force Command North was directed to breach the Iraqi defences in the centre of the Iraqi border. The Egyptian 3rd Mechanized Division spearheaded the advance.

The following day the two brigades of Smith's British 1st Armoured Division, preceded by Lynx attack helicopters, were to pour through the US 1st Infantry Division's breach. Swinging to the right, the British were to attack the Iraqi 12th Armoured Division, held in tactical reserve, in order to protect VII Corps' thrust towards the Republican Guard. This Iraqi division was estimated to number 13,000 men equipped with up to 300 T-55 and T-62 main battle tanks.

At 1515 hours on 25 February the 'Desert Rats' of Brigadier Cordingley's 7th Armoured Brigade, spearheading the British 1st Armoured Division, began to advance into Iraq, passing through the US lines. They were to thrust eastwards into Kuwait. Facing them were elements of the Iraqi 12th Armoured Division, which was now believed to be about 65 per cent combat effective: of its 250 tanks, only 115 remained operational. However, it was anticipated that the Iraqi 12th and 48th Divisions would remain in place, supported by an unidentified Iraqi brigade. It was clear that the going would not be easy.

Attacking a series of objectives codenamed after metals, the brigade destroyed two Iraqi tanks at 'Copper', a position believed to be defended by fourteen enemy tanks. The British Challengers' 120mm guns accounted for at least five further Iraqi T-55s and six APCs. Moving on to 'Zinc', a position that was thought to contain an Iraqi brigade with up to a hundred tanks, the 7th Armoured Brigade attacked in the darkness. All the Iraqis could do was fire back at the muzzle flashes as they counter-attacked with almost fifty vehicles. Daybreak revealed another ten Iraqi armoured vehicles knocked out in the desert sands.

On the night of 25/26 February Brigadier Christopher Hammerbeck's British 4th Armoured Brigade was also involved in a confused engagement with about twenty Iraqi tanks for 'Copper South'. The next day, with the 4th Brigade continuing its advance to the south, the 7th Brigade pressed on and the Iraqis lost another nine T-55s to British gunnery. Meanwhile, Hammerbeck's 4th Armoured Brigade attacked 'Brass', accounting for thirty tanks and almost fifty APCs; in total, it knocked out sixty MBTs and ninety APCs. During Desert Sabre the 1st Armoured Division accounted overall for 200 Iraqi T-62s, 100 AFVs and 100 artillery pieces. British Army Air Corps Lynx helicopters also destroyed at least four T-55s and seven other armoured vehicles, with a number of other probable hits. This said much for the superior British training and firepower.

A British Scorpion Combat Vehicle Reconnaissance (Tracked) of the 7th Armoured Brigade, 1st Armoured Division, advances east into Kuwait from southern Iraq during Operation Desert Storm.

The British Challenger tank first saw action during Desert Storm with the 'Desert Rats' of the 7th Armoured Brigade, which formed part of the British 1st Armoured Division.

A British 155mm howitzer. Britain deployed five regiments of artillery, including the 40th Field Regiment RA, which had twenty-four M109s capable of firing a 95lb high explosive shell 17.5km.

A British Scorpion armed with a 76mm gun. This vehicle was used by the British 1st Armoured Division's battlegroups for reconnaissance purposes, whilst the 16th/5th Lancers were equipped with Scimitars, a similar vehicle mounting a 30mm Rarden cannon, and Strikers, which fired Swingfire guided anti-tank missiles.

An FV432 armoured personnel carrier serving with the 'Desert Rats'. Note the sand being churned up. The 1960s vintage GKN Defence FV432 tracked APC took part in Desert Storm; as in the case of the Warrior, an air conditioning system was developed but not in time to see action. The FV432, capable of carrying ten men as well as the crew, replaced the Alvis Saracen 6x6 APC in 1963 and has since been supplemented by the Warrior.

A British Warrior Mechanized Combat Repair Vehicle with the 7th Armoured Brigade, 1st Armoured Division. The crew have dubbed it 'Abyss', and it also bears the 'desert rat' logo. Sandbags have been piled on to the front of the hull for added protection.

A Challenger crew from the Royal Scots Dragoon Guards taking a rest during a lull in the fighting. The Challenger's 120mm gun could knock out enemy tanks at 2,500 yards and beyond, and its excellent thermal sights allowed the crew to fight just as effectively at night. Its Chobham armour was enhanced by the addition of extra armour packs on the front and sides. In the background (*left to right*) can be seen an FV432 ambulance, an M548 Rapier missile supply vehicle and a Warrior (beyond the garbage truck).

British Warrior Infantry Fighting Vehicles poised for battle. Warriors were capable of carrying seven fully equipped infantrymen, and, as on the Challengers, extra armour was added to the sides and front for additional protection. During Desert Storm six variants of the Warrior were deployed, including the Artillery Observation and Battery Command vehicles that were seeing service for the first time.

A British Challenger stands guard over an American column.

This Iraqi T-72 main battle tank was destroyed in a coalition attack near the Ali Al Salem air base. US tank crews reported that the M1A1's thermal sights enabled them to acquire Iraqi targets through the smoke from oil well fires and other obscurants. The T-72 did not have the same advantage.

Two British Warriors supported by a recovery vehicle.

The Basra–Kuwait Highway near Kuwait City after the Iraqis had fled north. In the background are various British armoured personnel carriers, including two ambulances, and in the foreground is a loaded Iraqi ZPU-4 anti-aircraft gun.

The crew of this Iraqi T-72 made a fine job of camouflaging their vehicle, as well as adding sandbags for extra protection, but it did them no good. US tank crews reported that the M829A1 tank round was extremely effective against the T-72.

Chapter Nine

The Highway of Death

Once the ground war commenced, Iraqi troops quickly decided to abandon Kuwait and retreat behind the Republican Guard screen. The US Marines' feints had convinced them that they also faced an amphibious assault from the Gulf that would turn their flank. The Iraqis' flight from Kuwait City began on the night of 25 February, and the roads north to Basra soon became choked with massive numbers of fleeing vehicles. The next day about a thousand Iraqi vehicles on Highway 80 were destroyed by air strikes after the Muttla Pass was blocked.

The SAAF and Kuwaiti forces were almost in Kuwait City by 26 February, heralding the beginning of the end for the remains of the Iraqi Army in the KTO. The US Marines were on the outskirts, whilst XVIII Corps was in the Euphrates Valley and VII Corps was making progress against the Republican Guard. Nonetheless, units of an Iraqi armoured division decided to stand and fight in Kuwait City, perhaps with the express intention of buying time for their retreating comrades.

Liberation of the city followed a large-scale tank battle at the international airport. During the fighting the Iraqi 3rd Armoured Division (a veteran not only of the Iran–Iraq War but also the 1973 Arab–Israeli Yom Kippur War) lost over a hundred tanks. The US 1st Marine Division destroyed 310 Iraqi tanks in total across Kuwait. Iraqi defences had now all but collapsed, as it became every man for himself. The coalition victory was soon tainted by allegations that the fleeing Iraqis were needlessly massacred. Despite the media's lurid claims of a 'turkey shoot', most of the vehicles on Highway 80 – the 'highway of death' – were abandoned. Brigadier Patrick Cordingley recalled, 'There were not thousands of bodies, as the media claimed, but certainly hundreds; it was a reminder to all of us of the horror of war.'

Photographs of Highway 80 and the Muttla Pass showed that the bulk of the vehicles caught on the road were in fact stolen civilian cars, minibuses, pick-up trucks and tanker lorries; there was even a fire engine. The few military vehicles on the highway included several Brazilian Engesa EE-9 Cascavel armoured cars (Iraq had obtained 250 Cascavels during the 1980s, but it is not known how many were committed to the fighting in 1990–91), some army lorries and fuel trucks, and a tank transporter carrying an unidentified armoured vehicle. The most vivid and publicly damaging image was Kenneth Jarecke's photo of the completely charred head and shoulders of an Iraqi soldier leaning through the windscreen of his burnt-out vehicle. In the public's mind it had been a shameful massacre, rather than a defeated army receiving its just desserts.

Although the media had a field day with the horrific images from Highway 80, very few photos emerged of knocked-out Iraqi armour, and most of those examples that were depicted were old Iraqi T-55s. For example, at the end of February 1991 a T-55 was found on fire after being hit by a US 82nd Airborne Division anti-tank missile. Likewise, in early March an entrenched T-55 was shown burning behind its sand berm as a coalition lorry sped past.

British Centurion AVREs (Armoured Vehicle Royal Engineers) of the 1st Armoured Division were sent to help clear the charred debris from the Kuwait–Basra road, and two were photographed brushing aside a lorry and a car. About two dozen of these fifty-year-old veterans were used to deal with Saddam's anti-tank berms as Britain had nothing newer. Two were destroyed in a fire and one has since found its way into the safekeeping of the UK's Cobbaton Combat Collection (coincidentally the collection also has a GS 1 tonne 4x4 Rover, which is believed to have seen service with an artillery unit during Desert Storm, and a Ferret Mk2/3 4x4 scout car in Gulf War markings).

In truth, there was no 'Mother of Battles', as Saddam had threatened. Coalition forces only fought about 35 per cent of those Iraqi troops assessed to be in-theatre. The front echelon conscripts of Saddam's army were evidently expendable, whilst his loyal Republican Guard units largely managed to slink away with their bruised tails between their legs, to wreak more havoc in the months following the cease-fire.

What happened to Iraq's half a million troops in the KTO? Having spent six weeks pinned down by Desert Storm's relentless air attacks, Iraqi morale was at rock bottom and desertion rife. The western media played its part. Images of the 'Basra Pocket', Highway 80 and the Muttla Pass were seared into the western psyche, giving the impression that the battle for Kuwait City had all but crushed the Iraqi Army, making an honourable cease-fire an imperative. But were Saddam's regular army and Republican Guard really as soundly defeated as the West believed, or had the Coalition been chasing shell-shocked stragglers whilst the bulk of the Iraqi forces fled north in terror?

Rather than the 540,000 men initially assessed to be in the KTO, it is now believed they actually numbered about 250,000 (about 150,000 of them inside Kuwait). It has been estimated that there were probably only 100,000–200,000 men in theatre when the ground war started. These discrepancies in the figures were due to Saddam deploying a large number of under-strength divisions to give the impression that his forces were stronger than they really were. Washington claimed there were forty-three Iraqi divisions in the KTO, though western media sources only ever identified thirty-five.

Casualties for the Coalition were remarkably light. For example, America lost 148 killed in action and some 340 wounded; in addition, there were also almost 100 non-combat fatalities. The British lost thirty-six dead (seventeen of them in combat), and forty-three wounded. Friendly fire was a major contributor to the combat losses, with as many as thirty-five US personnel killed and seventy-two wounded by their own side. Likewise, nine British personnel were killed and thirteen wounded in unfortunate friendly fire incidents.

The debris of defeat. Two Iraqi T-55 tanks abandoned on the Basra–Kuwait highway near Kuwait City. It appears that the crews simply drove them off the road and then fled. The purpose of the oil drums is unclear: they either carried spare fuel or were used to generate smokescreens.

An abandoned Iraqi T-55A on the side of the road into Kuwait City. It appears undamaged.

This destroyed Iraqi T-55, dubbed 'Soviet made shit' by coalition troops, lies amidst the vast column of abandoned vehicles along the Kuwait City highway.

More abandoned cars and trucks clog the Basra–Kuwait highway out of Kuwait City after the retreat of Iraqi forces during Operation Desert Storm. In the foreground is an Iraqi DShKM 12.7mm anti-aircraft gun mounted on a tank turret.

Rocket-prcpelled grenades and other ordnance on Highway 80, the route that the fleeing Iraqi forces took as they retreated from Kuwait.

(*Above*) More debris left by the Iraqis fleeing from Kuwait. Note the solitary tank lying sandwiched in amongst the cars. The Muttla Ridge was where part of the Iraqi Army of Occupation was annihilated as it fled Kuwait City; one US general controversially dubbed it 'an execution'.

(*Opposite, top*) A burnt-out civilian car and an Iraqi T-55 tank on the Basra–Kuwait highway. This was the scene of one of the final coalition attacks as Iraqi forces retreated from Kuwait City.

(*Opposite, bottom*) Another casualty of war: this knocked out Iraqi T-54/55 was wrecked on the outskirts of Kuwait City. Judging by its position, it was attempting to escape from an air attack.

A Kuwaiti M-84 tank during Operation Desert Shield. In 1984 Yugoslavia began to build the Soviet T-72 main battle tank under licence as the M-84. The M-84A was the version obtained by Kuwait, and featured an up-armoured turret and hull similar to the Russian T-72M1. The M84 was superior to the Kuwaiti's Chieftains. It was lighter and therefore easier to manoeuvre, was equipped with a computer and fire control system, and was fitted with a 125mm gun capable of firing armour-piercing and shaped charges.

Kuwaiti soldiers sitting beside an Iraqi BMP-2 mechanized infantry combat vehicle that was captured during Operation Desert Storm. The vehicle has an AT-5 Spandrel anti-tank guided missile mounted atop its turret.

Chapter Ten

The Basra Pocket

While the Coalition fought to free Kuwait City, up to 800 American tanks from the US VII Corps' 1st and 3rd Armored Divisions and the 2nd Armoured Cavalry Regiment launched attacks on a Republican Guard division inside Iraq, which lost 200 tanks. They then moved forwards and engaged a second division. American Apache attack helicopters and A-10 Thunderbolt tank-busters also played a significant role. One Apache alone destroyed eight T-72s, and on 25 February two USAF A-10s destroyed twenty-three Iraqi tanks, including some T-72s, in three close air support missions.

In the envelopment the US M1A1 tanks easily outgunned the Iraqi T-72s, and in a night engagement on 25/26 February the Guards' Tawakalna Armoured Division was largely destroyed without the loss of a single US tank. The Republican Guard, unable to stem the American armoured tide, tried to retreat, and the next morning a brigade of the Medina Division, supported by a battalion from the 14th Mechanized Division, attempted to protect the withdrawal. The Medina troops found themselves under attack from the US 1st and 3rd Armored Divisions, while the remnants of the Tawakalna were finished off by air attacks.

Caught as they were being loaded onto their tank transporters, the Medina Division's armoured vehicles were bombed by USAF A-10s and F-16 fighters. Apache attack helicopters caught another eighty T-72 tanks still on their transporters along Route 8. Although not all the roads out of Basra were closed, the Coalition was determined that Iraqi tanks and artillery should not escape. The US VII Corps' armour also fought the Hammurabi Republican Guard Division 80km to the west of Basra.

The US 24th Mechanized Division, having made a dramatic 150-mile drive northwards to join the US 101st Airborne Division on the Euphrates, now swung to the right to block the Iraqi escape route. The six remaining Republican Guard divisions had been trapped overnight in a swiftly diminishing area of northern Kuwait and southern Iraq, with their northward line of escape largely severed.

On 27 February the US 24th Mechanized Division attacked the Guard's Hammurabi Armoured Division, the al-Faw and Adnan Infantry Divisions and the remnants of the Nebuchadnezzar Infantry Division. They fled, with the Nebuchadnezzar Division possibly escaping over the Hawr al-Hammar Lake causeway. The 24th Mechanized Division also captured fifty Republican Guard T-72 tanks as they were fleeing north along a main road near the Euphrates. It was all but over for the Guards.

Six disparate brigades with fewer than 30,000 troops and a few tanks were now struggling back to Basra. The Iraqis agreed to a cease-fire the following day, whilst the British 7th Armoured Brigade moved to cut the road to Basra just north of Kuwait City. However, some troops continued to escape across the Hawr al-Hammar and north from Basra along the Shatt al-Arab Waterway. Brigadier Cordingley, Commander of the 7th Armoured Brigade, noted, 'By 28 February it was clear that General Schwarzkopf's plan to annihilate the Republican Guard with a left hook through Iraq had failed . . . The majority of the Iraqi soldiers were already on their way back to Baghdad.'

Firmly in control of Iraq's state media, Saddam had no need to acknowledge this terrible defeat, and instead victory was given as the reason for abiding by the cease-fire. Baghdad Radio announced, 'The Mother of battles was a clear victory for Iraq . . . We are happy with the cessation of combat operations as this would preserve our sons' blood and people's safety after God made them triumphant with faith against their evil enemies.'

Only a residual Iraqi threat remained by 30 February. Two Iraqi tank brigades were south-west of Basra, another brigade with forty armoured vehicles was to the south and an infantry brigade was on either side of the Hawr al-Hammar Lake. In total, about eight armoured battalions, the remnants of those Iraqi forces deployed in and around Kuwait, were now trapped in the 'Basra Pocket'. Basra itself lay in ruins, and marshes and wetlands to the west and east made passage impossible.

Despite the cease-fire, the US 24th Division fought elements of the Hammurabi Division again on 2 March after reports that a battalion of T-72 tanks was moving northwards towards it in an effort to escape. The Iraqi armoured column foolishly opened fire and suffered the consequences. The Americans retaliated with Apache attack helicopters and two task forces, destroying 187 armoured vehicles, 34 artillery pieces and 400 trucks. The survivors were forced back into the 'Basra Pocket'. By this stage Iraq only had about 700 of its 4,500 tanks and 1,000 of its 2,800 APCs left in the KTO and, with organized resistance over, the Iraqis signed the cease-fire on 3 March 1991.

In the wake of Desert Sabre, only the Iraqi Army Air Corps and the Republican Guard Corps secured favour with Saddam Hussein, by swiftly crushing the revolt in the south against his regime and containing the resurgent Kurds in the north. In contrast the Iraqi Army and Iraqi Air Force had fled Desert Storm and remained under a cloud. Subsequently the IrAF found itself grounded by the Coalition's cease-fire terms, while the army was left face to face with the barrels of the Republican Guard Corps' remaining tanks. After a brief stand-off, the Iraqi Army opted for the status quo, but its loyalty and competence remained tarnished by its collapse and by the actions of thousands of deserters.

In 1991 the Coalition accounted for just six Iraqi helicopters (one Mi-8, one BO-105 and four unidentified) in the air and another five on the ground. General Schwarzkopf had cause to regret that they did not destroy more. During the cease-fire talks on 3 March 1991 the Iraqis requested that, in light of the damage done to their infrastructure, they be allowed to move government officials around by helicopter. Without fully realizing the consequences, Schwarzkopf agreed not to shoot down 'any' helicopters flying over Iraqi territory. Thus, by using his helicopter gunships Saddam was able to crush the rebellion in Iraq's cities and the southern marshes and Kurdish advances in the north with impunity, despite his defeat in Kuwait.

In hindsight, Schwarzkopf felt that grounding Iraqi helicopters would have made little difference. In his view the Iraqi armour and artillery of the twenty-four remaining divisions, which had never entered the war zone, had a far more devastating impact on the rebels. This was a little disingenuous, for while tanks and artillery were instrumental in crushing the revolts in the predominantly Shia cities of Basra, Karbala and Najaf (the scene of Shi'ite unrest in 1977, resulting in 2,000 Shia arrests and another 200,000 being expelled to Iran), in the southern marshes the Republican Guard's T-72 tanks could not operate off the causeways and artillery was only effective against pre-spotted targets. In fact the Iraqi Army Air Corps played a pivotal role over Iraq's rebellious cities, the southern marches and the Kurdish mountains.

Over the cities helicopter gunships were used indiscriminately to machine gun and rocket the civilian population in order to break their morale. Although there was no evidence of the use of chemical weapons (Saddam did not want to provoke further coalition intervention so stayed his hand), on at least one occasion residential areas were reportedly sprayed with sulphuric acid. This was corroborated by French military units still in southern Iraq, who treated Iraqi refugees with severe acid burns.

Although the rebellion was mainly a spontaneous outburst by defeated and disaffected troops returning home, its religious Shia basis meant that it was ultimately doomed. America stood by, as a Shia victory would only serve radical Shia Iran, and as a result the rebels did not even receive airdrops of manportable anti-aircraft and anti-tank missiles with which to fend off Saddam's helicopters and tanks. The Iraqi military, dominated by the Sunni minority, went about their business unhindered.

After authority had been brutally reasserted in the cities, thousands fled into Iraq's southern marshes seeking sanctuary. Here the IAAC was even more instrumental in the destruction of those forlorn forces that the West had vaguely hoped would unseat Saddam. IAAC pilots knew what lay in store for them if they failed, as General Ali Hassan al-Majid, who was commanding the operation, warned at least pilot not to return unless he had wiped out some insurgents obstructing a bridge.

The whole operation in the marshes was largely a repeat of March 1984, when Iraqi helicopter gunships mercilessly hunted Iranian troops round the two important Majnoon Island oil facilities. This time they refrained from using mustard gas or any other chemical agents, but once again the unburied dead were left to become carrion for the jackals, and those foolish enough to surrender were shot at point-blank range. The IAAC contributed to the deaths of an estimated 30,000 rebels. Additionally 3,000 Shia clerics were driven from Najaf and fled to the Iranian town of Qom.

In the north the fear of another Halabja was sufficient to scatter the Kurdish population at the first sight of an aircraft. The IrAF and IAAC once more refrained from deploying chemical weapons, but callously contented themselves with dropping flour on the refugees, who instantly panicked. Once more the Iraqi military made use of their helicopters and artillery to eject the lightly armed Kurdish guerrillas from their recent conquests.

Whilst the IAAC had continued to fly after 1991, in defiance of the cease-fire terms the IrAF resumed operational and training flights with its fixed-wing aircraft in April 1992. The IrAF claimed it was responding to the provocation of an Iranian Air Force attack on an Iranian opposition force's base east of Baghdad. In response to these violations, and the repressive military operations, the UN imposed two separate no-fly zones in the north and south of the country.

Due to UN sanctions and financial restrictions, the Iraqi Air Force could only manage about a hundred sorties per day, down from 800 in the heyday of the Iran–Iraq War. Residual IrAF capabilities remained in the Baghdad, Mosul and Kirkuk areas, protecting Saddam from dissidents and the Kurds. Throughout most of the 1990s the IrAF spent much of its time dodging the northern and southern no-fly zones, though at least two fighters (a MiG-23 and a MiG-25) were lost for violating these zones.

An M1A1 Abrams of the 3rd Brigade, 1st Armored Division, US 7th Corps, moves across the desert in northern Kuwait during Operation Desert Sabre. The US 1st and 3rd Armored Divisions launched attacks on a Republican Guard division inside Iraq, which lost 200 tanks.

More armour from the US 1st Armored Division. In the envelopment of the Republican Guard in the Basra pocket, the US M1A1 tank easily outgunned the Iraqi T-72. Seven separate M1A1 crews reported being hit by T-72 tank rounds; the Abrams sustained no damage, however, attesting to the effectiveness of the US Army's heavy armour.

A US M48 Chaparral low-altitude, self-propelled, surface-to-air missile system during Desert Storm.

There was no escape for these Iraqi BMP-1s. When the Republican Guard tried to retreat, its rearguard Medina Division was overwhelmed, along with the Tawakalna Division.

US Marines with a captured Iraqi BMP-1.

Adorned with graffiti by Coalition troops, this wrecked Iraqi T-55, together with a supply truck that seems to have run into the back of it, stands on the highway between Kuwait City and Basra.

An Iraqi tank amidst Kuwait's burning oilfields.

The final resting place for an Iraqi Type 69. Iraq lost up to 4,000 tanks during Desert Storm, mostly to air strikes.

The 'Abyss' Warrior recovery vehicle parked in front of some British Challengers (*left*) and Challenger recovery vehicles.

Iraq's Soviet- and Chinese-supplied tanks proved to be all but useless in the face of the Coalition's overwhelming firepower.

Chapter Eleven

The Reckoning

Following Operation Desert Storm/Desert Sabre no conclusive body-count was ever issued. Washington estimated that over 100,000 Iraqis were killed and 300,000 wounded, with another 175,000 taken prisoner. However, these figures add up to a total far greater than the number of men originally assessed to be in the KTO. British estimates were much more conservative, with 30,000 Iraqi dead and 100,000 wounded. The air war alone was initially thought to have accounted for 100,000, but when the fighting was over this figure was revised to 10,000. The Iraqis themselves claimed they had lost 20,000 dead and 60,000 wounded in twenty-six days of air attacks. It has also since been estimated that just 10,000 Iraqis were killed during the land offensive. Despite this, a total of 20,000–30,000 dead seems rather high, and a conservative estimate of less than 10,000 remains more likely.

The irony is that, because his forces held their ground during the protracted preliminary air campaign, the ground war, although brief, ensured Saddam Hussein got a favourable cease-fire outcome (i.e. the coalition forces just 240km away did not press on to Baghdad, and he stayed in power). The loyal Republican Guard remained reasonably intact; they had lost their tanks but not their will to fight for Saddam, meaning that he was easily able to crush the Iraqi revolts that took place once the cease-fire was secure. Schwarzkopf admitted that a substantial Iraqi force was still left north of the Tigris–Euphrates Valley, but although it was 'an infantry army, it's not an armoured army'.

Indeed, the surviving Iraqi armed forces could still constitute a sizeable army. After the war ended, Saddam still had perhaps 250,000 men under arms, equipped with 1,700 tanks (700 from the KTO and 1,000 still in Iraq), 6,700 APCs (1,400 from the KTO and 5,300 still in Iraq) and almost 800 pieces of artillery (340 from the KTO and 443 still in Iraq). There were seven divisions around Baghdad, plus forces on the Syrian border and about nine divisions on the Turkish border. There were two Republican Guard divisions in Baghdad, perhaps 24,000 men, with another five or so army divisions in the area, comprising another 60,000 men. Although south-western Iraq had been overrun, no Scud missiles were found, leaving an estimated 300 still posing a threat to Israel. For the best part of the next decade the UN Special

Commission for Iraq embarked on a wild goose chase hunting for Iraq's weapons of mass destruction.

Desert Sabre was a classic textbook offensive conducted with bravery, verve and professionalism by all those involved. In contrast, the Iraqi Army proved to be a house of cards. The Republican Guard Corps had been an unknown quantity: would they fight and if so how hard? Lieutenant William Ratliff of the US 1st Armored Division summed up the situation in the end: 'I think we overestimated [the enemy]. We were told the Republican Guard was the best [Saddam] had. We expected better.'

Before the ground offensive, the Coalition's combined air forces launched a round-the-clock air campaign, targeting Iraqi command and control sites, Scud missile installations, lines of communication, and the Republican Guard tanks and other vehicles. Vitally, air superiority over Kuwait and Iraq was achieved within twenty-four hours of the first air attacks. Some 35,000 air sorties were launched against Iraqi ground forces, of which 5,600 were directed at the Republican Guard.

According to American-derived figures, the Coalition destroyed or captured 5,297 armoured vehicles (3,847 tanks and 1,450 APCs), as well as 2,917 pieces of artillery (see table). One of the highest scores fell to the British 1st Armoured Division, which accounted for 400 tanks, AFVs and artillery pieces. British Army Air Corps' Lynx helicopters destroyed at least four T-55s and seven other armoured vehicles, with a number of other probable hits. Similarly the US 1st Marine Division claimed about 310 Iraqi tanks in and around Kuwait City. In total, Iraq's pre-war holdings of 10,687 tanks, APCs and artillery pieces had plummeted to 2,473.

Estimates of Iraqi military losses in 1991

Type	Pre-war holdings	Destroyed or captured	Remaining
Tanks	4,550	3,847	703
APCs	2,880	1,450	1,430
Artillery	3,257	2,917	340
Totals:	10,687	8,214	2,473

In his account of the Gulf War General de la Billiere wrote:

The rules of the game are that the victor is allowed to keep captured military equipment from the area over which he has advanced . . . The rest they [7th Brigade] had blown up and destroyed, to prevent the Iraqis getting it. Norman Schwarzkopf and I had issued strict orders to our forces that they were to retrace their routes of advance during the battle and make sure that nothing serviceable was left behind. The operation of identifying, recovering or destroying equipment went on for at least ten days after the end of the war.

The complete destruction of 400–800 military vehicles and pieces of artillery a day seems an impossibility. What is more, this captured equipment lay *inside* Iraq, and the Iraqis, masters of invention, were able collect some, if not much, of it and restore it or cannibalize it for spare parts. Similarly the 175,000 PoWs were repatriated.

After the ground war came to a close, samples of Iraq's armoured forces were gathered up for intelligence exploitation, ending up at Britain's Defence Research Agency at Chertsey, and America's National Ground Intelligence Centre at Charlottesville and the Aberdeen Proving Ground. The Coalition captured numerous Chinese and Soviet armoured vehicle types, including the Chinese Type 69-II with a laser range-finder fitted over the mantlet of the 100mm gun (Iraq is believed to have imported over 1,000 Type 69 and 59 tanks), and Type 653 recovery vehicles (based on the Type 69 chassis).

Some of the more unusual armoured vehicles to be captured in Kuwait included the Soviet BMD-1 airborne combat vehicle and the French Panhard M3 APC. Iraq had only a few BMDs, and why they were deployed to Kuwait is unclear; the M3s, of which France had supplied 200, were veterans of the Iran–Iraq War and by 1990 remaining numbers were uncertain.

Not inconsiderable numbers of artillery pieces were captured. For example, whole batteries of Soviet-supplied 2S3 152mm self-propelled guns were overrun and some M-46 130mm field guns were found abandoned in their sandbagged firing positions. The Coalition also captured Chinese Type 83 152mm and Type 59-1 130mm field guns and Yugoslav-supplied M56 105mm howitzers.

Britain's Tank Museum acquired a Chinese-built Type 69-II main battle tank, a Chinese Type YW-701 command post vehicle (based on the YW-531 and deployed by regimental and divisional commanders) and several Type YW-750 ambulances (Iraq imported an estimated total of 500 Norinco YW-531 APCs in the early 1980s), as well as a Soviet up-armoured T-55, a BMP and a 2S3 152mm self-propelled gun. (Iraq also fielded the 2S4 240mm self-propelled mortar and 2S1 122mm self-propelled howitzer.)

At least one vehicle park contained approximately 150–200 mainly Soviet-origin armoured vehicles, including about forty tanks. Amongst the mangled debris were Soviet BMP infantry fighting vehicles, MT-LBs, and T-54 and T-62 tanks. There were other such collections scattered throughout the Iraqi desert, but the numbers seemed to belie the 5,297 claimed. Additionally, there seemed to be a discrepancy in the ratio of tanks to APCs destroyed, with far more tanks claimed.

It is not clear how these figures were derived: it remains uncertain whether they were based on air strike and tank kill claims, or the Coalition simply took an average area and multiplied the debris to create an aggregate total, or they physically counted every single vehicle on the battlefield (which seems unlikely). There was clearly some double-counting by the ground and air forces as they conducted their Battle Damage Assessments, which were largely contradictory throughout the war. Vehicles rounded up for exploitation were numbered or lettered, but again it is not clear if the numbers referred to the overall total, the particular vehicle type totals or were simply shipping numbers.

Naturally, not all Iraq's destroyed and abandoned AFVs turned out to be the real thing. Saddam's dummy tanks may have fooled the Coalition's air forces, but they were also a pathetic symbol of Iraq's ultimate battlefield weakness. Photo-journalist Gilles Sanssier saw one decoy that was simply a crude corrugated steel sheet rectangle with an oil drum and a pipe forming the turret. The whole thing was draped in a net to give the impression of camouflage. From the air the assumption was that it was a tank – from the ground it was risible.

Remarkably, during the whole of Desert Storm only four M1A1s were disabled and no Challenger 1s were lost to enemy action. The Challengers reportedly accounted for about 300 Iraqi armoured vehicles. The veteran Challenger 1 was replaced by Challenger 2 in 2001, with many of the earlier tanks being sold to Jordan. In March 1991 the US Department of Defense released the following glowing report regarding the performance of the M1A1 Abrams tank:

After 100 hours of offensive operations, the operational readiness rates of both the VII Corps and XVIII Airborne Corps exceeded the Army's 90 per cent standard. Especially noteworthy was a night move by the 3rd Armored Division covering 200km (120 miles). None of the more than 300 tanks in the division broke down.

Seven separate M1A1 crews reported being hit by T-72 tank rounds. These M1A1s sustained no damage, attesting to the effectiveness of our heavy armour. Other crews reported that the M1A1 thermal sight allowed them to acquire Iraqi T-72s through the smoke from oil well fires and other obscurants. The T-72 did not have the same advantage. This situation gave the Abrams a significant edge in survivability, engagement range and night manoeuvre. Additionally tank crews reported that the M829A1 tank round was extremely effective against the T-72. In sum, the combined performance of the Abrams armour, thermal sight and ammunition attest to the systems' exceptional lethality and survivability.

Of the 1,955 M1A1 Abrams tanks in theatre, four were disabled and four were damaged but are repairable. No M1A1 crew members were killed by enemy fire in the many tank engagements.

This was clearly a remarkable achievement.

Saddam had made good his threat to burn Kuwait if he was forced from it. In the aftermath of the liberation it was established that 798 wellheads had been detonated, of which 603 caught fire and 45 gushed oil. In addition, there were 100km of oil-filled trenches. Overall 62 million cubic metres of soil was contaminated and over a billion barrels of oil lost. There was both wet and dry oil ground contamination, along with a dreadful crust created by 'tarcrete', and scattered everywhere was abandoned ordnance of all shapes and sizes. All of this amounted to some $50 billion worth of damage. It was environmental vandalism on an unprecedented scale.

A Kuwaiti oil field set on fire by retreating Iraqi troops burns in the distance beyond an abandoned Iraqi tank. Saddam's troops caused $50bn worth of damage.

(*Above*) Blazing oil wells and spilt oil. An aerial view of the environmental vandalism wrought by the retreating Iraqis, who blew up almost 800 wellheads and wasted over a billion barrels of oil.

(*Opposite, top*) US F-16s and F-14s fly over Kuwait's burning oil wells.

(*Opposite, bottom*) Firefighters attempt to cap one of the 600 blazing Kuwaiti wellheads.

An Iraqi tank lies amongst Kuwait's destroyed oil fields. The smoke from the fires turned day into night.

Derelict Iraqi aircraft. Like most of Saddam's military equipment, these aircraft ended up as so much junk.

Two more shots of the 'Abyss'.

Egyptian troops stand ready for review by King Fahd of Saudi Arabia. Desert Storm witnessed unprecedented cooperation in the Arab world.

President Bush greets General H. Norman Schwarzkopf, leading the Desert Storm Homecoming Parade in Washington, D.C. In New York the coalition commander was honoured with a ticker-tape parade.

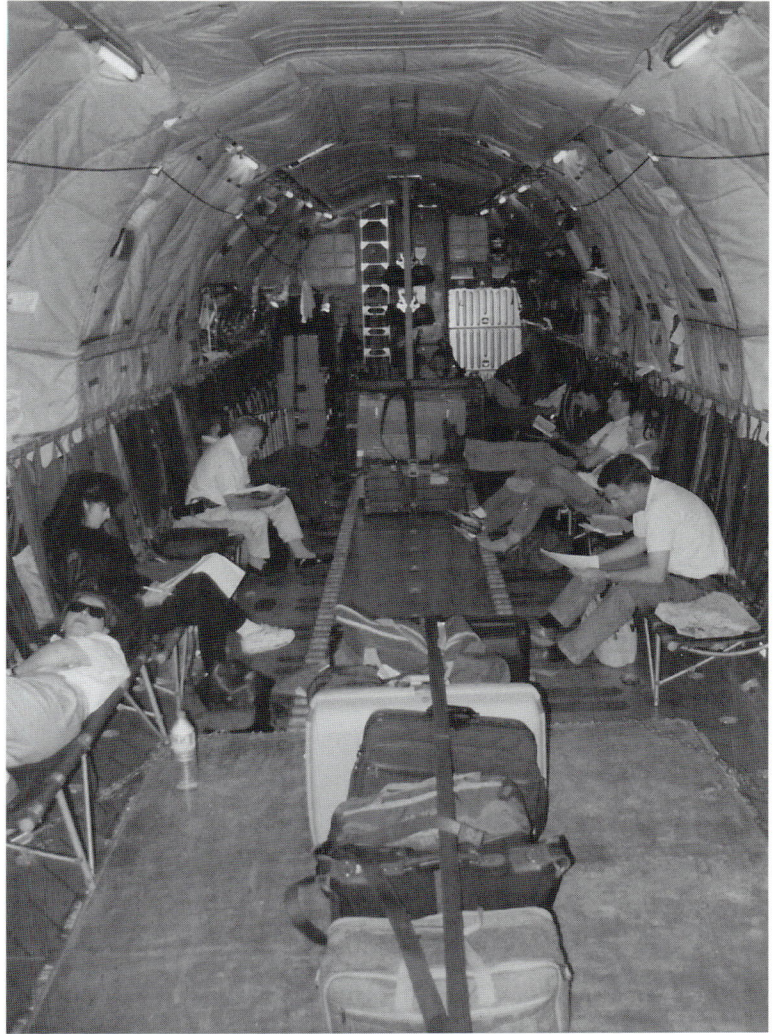

Following Operation Desert Storm, UNSCOM weapons inspectors moved into Iraq to dismantle Saddam Hussein's weapons of mass destruction.

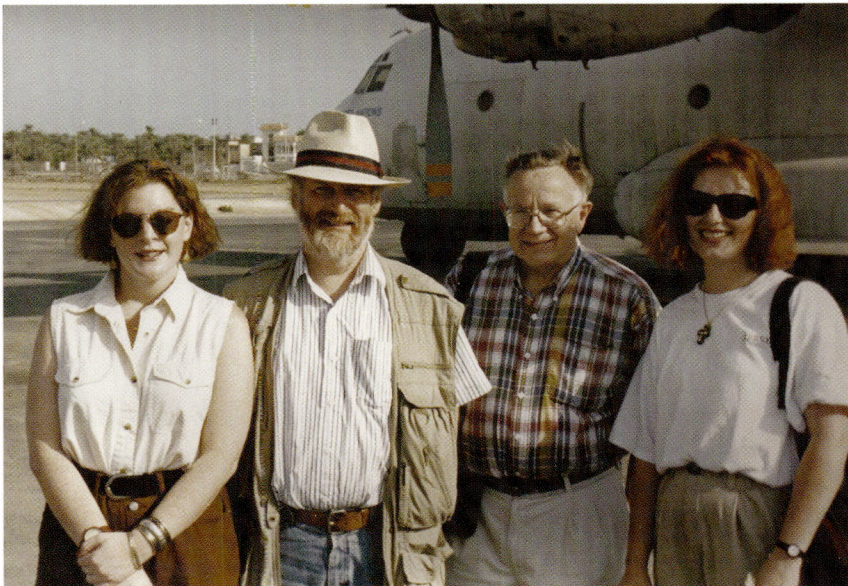

British, American and French UNSCOM inspectors. Second from the left is Dr David Kelly, who subsequently took his own life over the British government's handling of the 2003 Iraq War.

Epilogue

In the aftermath of the war the battered Iraqi Air Force made little attempt to make good the damage wrought on its infrastructure. In 1994, when the author was there, Habbaniyah air base west of Baghdad remained a junkyard of ruined buildings and scrap metal, and yet the Iraqis visibly continued to operate from it. Three years later it was not much better, when Richard Butler, head of the UN Special Commission for Iraq (UNSCOM), observed, 'It was a vast and desolate airfield dotted with military aircraft of many kinds and some tanks, almost all of Soviet origin. These machines were dirty and apparently in disrepair, but during our repeated flights in and out of Habbaniyah we would often see the fighter aircraft fly, mainly in "touch-and-go" [take-off and landing] exercises.'

In 1996 things came to a head when Saddam urged his air defence forces to ignore both no-fly zones and attack 'any air target of the aggressors'. These transgressions of the no-fly zones and Iraq's failure to comply with UNSCOM helped spark Operation Desert Fox two years later. American and British aircraft conducted a four-day bombardment of Iraqi targets, including air defence installations. This proved to be a failure as Iraq remained defiant and UNSCOM was expelled. The Iraqi Air Force and Air Defence Command (IADC) continued to taunt those aircraft, patrolling the no-fly zones largely with impunity. According to the US Joint Chiefs of Staff Chairman, Air Force General Richard Myers, over a three-year period Iraqi artillery fired at coalition aircraft more than 1,000 times, launched 600 rockets and fired nearly 60 surface-to-air missiles. During 2002 alone there were 406 firing incidents at patrolling aircraft.

In response, the coalition forces changed tactics. Instead of retaliating against AAA and SAM batteries, they began targeting the command, control and communications network of the IrAF and IADC. In an escalation of the confrontation in September 2002 coalition warplanes attacked five sites across southern Iraq, including an air defence communications installation near Tallil, 260km south-east of Baghdad. This was in response to the Iraqis again firing on patrolling aircraft and allegedly shooting down an American UAV in August.

The UN embargo ensured that the IrAF received no new aircraft, surface-to-air missiles or sensors (with the possible exception of French Matra Magic 2 short-range air-to-air missiles in 1996). After ten years of sanctions it was thought to still have 130 attack aircraft and 180 fighters, but only 90–100 aircraft were serviceable

– enough perhaps to counter any internal unrest but not the United States Air Force.

General Myers, in his testimony before the House Armed Services Committee on 18 September 2002, stated Iraq had about 300 aircraft, including a few Mirage F-1s and MiG-29s, though fewer than 50 per cent were mission capable, and more than fifty key air defence radars. Only the IAAC was believed to be in a reasonable condition, though reporters on a trip to Tuwaitha were treated to a show of the Iraqis' appalling helicopter maintenance standards. Resources had been allocated to the IADC, though its missiles, radars and support systems were out-of-date and unable to prevent continual American and British combat air patrols over the no-fly zones. Finally, in 2003 Operation Iraqi Freedom drove Saddam Hussein from power.*

---

* See The Iraq War, Operation Iraqi Freedom, 2003–2011, the companion volume in this series.

Suggested Further Reading

Billière,General Sir Peter de la, *Storm Command. A Personal Account of the Gulf War* (Harper Collins, London,1992)

Brown, Ben & Shukman, David, *All Necessary Means Inside the Gulf War* (BBC Books, London, 1991)

Bulloch, John & Morris, Harvey, *Saddam's War. The Origins of the Kuwait Conflict and the International Response* (Faber & Faber, London, 1991)

Chant, Christopher, *Air War in the Gulf 1991* (Osprey Publishing, Oxford, 2001)

Cordingley, Major General Patrick, *In the Eye of the Storm. Commanding the Desert Rats in the Gulf War* (Hodder & Stoughton, London, 1996)

Freedman, Lawrence & Karsh, Efraim, *The Gulf Conflict 1991* (Faber & Faber, London, 1993)

McNab, Andy, *Bravo Two Zero* (Bantam Press, London, 1993)

Munro, Alan, *Arab Storm. Politics and Diplomacy Behind the Gulf War* (I.B. Taurus, London, 2006)

Peters, John & Nichol, John, *Tornado Down* (Signet, London, 1993)

Rottman, Gordon & Volstad, Ron, *Armies of the Gulf War* (Osprey Publishing, London, 1993)

Ryan, Chris, *The One that Got Away* (Century, London, 1995)

Schwarzkopf, General H. Norman & Petre, Peter, *The Autobiography. It Doesn't Take A Hero* (Bantam Books, London, 1993)

Timmerman, Kenneth R., *The Death Lobby. How the West Armed Iraq* (Bantam Books, 1992)

Watson, Bruce W., George MP, Bruce, Tsouras, Peter, Cyr, B.L & the International Analysis Group on the Gulf War, *Military Lessons of the Gulf War* (Greenhill Books, London, 1991)